Quarterly Essay

Quarterly Essay is published four times a year by Black Inc., an imprint of Schwartz Publishing Pty Ltd. Publisher: Morry Schwartz.

ISBN 9781760641511 ISSN 1832-0953

Subscriptions – 1 year print & digital (4 issues): $79.95 within Australia incl. GST. Outside Australia $119.95. 2 years print & digital (8 issues): $149.95 within Australia incl. GST. 1 year digital only: $49.95.

Payment may be made by Mastercard or Visa, or by cheque made out to Schwartz Publishing. Payment includes postage and handling.

To subscribe, fill out and post the subscription card or form inside this issue, or subscribe online:

quarterlyessay.com
subscribe@blackincbooks.com
Phone: 61 3 9486 0288

Correspondence should be addressed to:

The Editor, Quarterly Essay
Level 1, 221 Drummond Street
Carlton VIC 3053 Australia
Phone: 61 3 9486 0288 / Fax: 61 3 9011 6106
Email: quarterlyessay@blackincbooks.com

Editor: Chris Feik. Management: Caitlin Yates. Publicity: Anna Lensky. Design: Guy Mirabella. Assistant Editor: Kirstie Innes-Will. Production Coordinator: Marilyn de Castro. Typesetting: Akiko Chan.

Printed in Australia by McPherson's Printing Group. The paper used to produce this book comes from wood grown in sustainable forests.

For Evelyn, who needs the world to change

THE PROSPERITY GOSPEL

How Scott Morrison won and Bill Shorten lost

Erik Jensen

> A special virtue attaches to plays which remind the drama of how much it can do without and still exist.
>
> —Kenneth Tynan

SOUR CHEESECAKE

The first staffer says it just before eight o'clock: "We're fucked. Yep, completely fucked."

The swings in Queensland are coming through. Herbert is gone. "It's like Hillary at 3 p.m. on that awful night," a staffer says, "when everything would just have to go right if there's any hope."

Shorten's election party is held in the function room of an airport hotel. On one side of the building is an industrial estate and on the other is the airfield. In the corners, balloons are clustered like grapes. The lights burn pink on people's skin. Outside, the moon is unusually large.

Early on there's a good feeling in Braddon. It looks as if they're ahead in Corangamite. A staffer says that if they hold in Tasmania, win Corangamite and hold Lindsay, there's no way the Liberals can keep government.

"Just put me out for an hour," he says, "and wake me up when it's done."

Anthony Pratt arrives, wearing a Prada jacket. His father was close with Shorten. The richest man in Australia doesn't know quite where to stand. "He's been very good," Pratt says. "He's done it with great aplomb. The NDIS and those guys down in the mine. They say there's no small parts, just small actors. And Bill's not a small actor. He's just a great talent. There are some things you need talent for and I think Bill's got that immense talent."

Trays of party pies are offered around. Very quickly, there is the feeling of a wake, only without the warmth or fond stories. Barnaby Joyce wins comfortably and the room boos. There are long, sad faces. People's eyes are underlined with resignation.

Tony Abbott is making a concession speech. He has lost to Zali Steggall, an independent. He claims the evening as a victory for the Coalition. "Where climate change is a moral issue, we Liberals do it tough," he says. "But where climate change is an economic issue, the Liberals do well."

Longman in Queensland is lost on One Nation preferences. The Liberals have won Bass in Tasmania. By nine o'clock the room has emptied by a third. People look hollowed out. The wait staff bring out platters of sour-tasting cheesecake. "This is a terrible night," a staffer says. "Fucking terrible."

At 9.30, Antony Green calls it for the Coalition. Peter Dutton quotes Paul Keating: "This is the sweetest victory of all." People's jackets smell more and more of cigarettes. The air smells of wine and warm breath.

On the screen, Scott Morrison makes his way to the side of stage. Bronwyn Bishop is there and when she hugs him her nails look like red beetles on his back. He shakes hands with Philip Ruddock and then John Howard. This is the party he has got back together.

Morrison's forehead glistens under the lights. His first line as returned prime minister is religious: "I have always believed in miracles."

At the Labor function, they cut the sound. The corners of Morrison's mouth twist as he forms silent words. He is thanking the quiet people who have won him this victory. Just after midnight, Bill Shorten's bus pulls out from the back of the hotel and disappears into the darkness.

ONE MORNING IN APRIL

The cyclamens are indifferent. Their faces are pink and beautiful, turned downwards against the cold. It is Thursday and Scott Morrison is in the prime minister's courtyard. He is announcing an election.

"Earlier this morning, I visited the governor-general here in Canberra," he says, "and he accepted my advice for an election to be held on the 18th of May."

As he talks, Morrison holsters his thumb in the crook of his forefinger. He rocks on his feet and the shoulders of his jacket shift independently of his head. "We live in the best country in the world," he says, "but to secure your future, the road ahead depends on a strong economy, and that's why there is so much at stake at this election."

He promises, again, a surplus. He says one and a quarter million jobs will be created in the next five years.

"We will maintain those budget surpluses without increasing taxes, and pay down the debt," he says. "We will deliver tax relief, as we have, for families, for hard-working Australians, for small businesses, allowing Australians to keep more of what they earn. We will keep Australians safe, as Liberal–National governments always do. And we will keep our borders secure, as you know we will. And we will be able to guarantee the increased funding for the essential services that Australians rely on. Schools, hospitals, medicines, roads – all guaranteed by a stronger economy."

Morrison has the face of a man delivering bad news, not yet certain how bad it really is. His eyes are curtained with seriousness. His voice dips at the end of each phrase, like a mourner bowing his head before going into church.

"There is more to do and a lot has got done, and we are getting on together with the job," he says. "So at this election there is a clear choice. It is a choice that will determine the economy that Australians live in, not just for the next three years but for the next decade. It's a choice between a government that I lead and the alternative of a Labor government led by

Bill Shorten. You will have the choice between a government that is delivering a strong economy and will continue to do so, or Bill Shorten's Labor Party, whose policies would weaken our economy. You will get to decide between a government that has fixed the budget or Bill Shorten's Labor Party, that we always know can't manage money. You will have a choice between a government that is lowering taxes for all Australians, or Bill Shorten's Labor Party, that will impose higher taxes that will weigh down our economy. It's taken us more than five years to turn around Labor's budget mess. Now is not the time to turn back."

Morrison says he believes in a fair go for those who have a go. He says that is part of the promise made by all Australians, to make a contribution and not seek to take one. The phrases bring satisfaction to his face. He enjoys repetition. He is pleased by rhyme.

He says this is an election about the future. He promises not much. He points again to the economy, to national security and to border protection. There is nothing new here. The speech is an appeal to the recent past, and a hope to continue living there.

He says the election is about who you trust to manage the economy. He says that is what every election is about. He says a strong economy is the path to higher wages. He talks about the champion in all Australians. He says he plans to release those champions, in homes and hospitals and workplaces. "Make no mistake," he says. "Elections are all about questions of trust and our record of delivery on the things that Australians rely on, the economy they live in and the services that they rely on is very clear and our plans to continue to deliver that are very clear."

A new phrase occurs to him, and the neatness of it opens his face a little. "It's crystal-clear, at this election," he says. "It is a choice between me as prime minister and Bill Shorten as prime minister. You vote for me, you'll get me. You vote for Bill Shorten and you'll get Bill Shorten."

It takes just on twelve minutes. The parliament is dissolved half an hour before government science agencies are due to answer questions about the mine approval given to Adani two days earlier.

*

It is a cold, early day and the sky has the character of painted china. The election is two weeks from being called. At the takeaway across the road from his office, Bill Shorten asks the woman serving if anything on the menu is good.

He says he doesn't like to speak in the first person. "I hate using the 'I' word."

He says it's not about him. He says he feels more passionate than he ever has, more optimistic. He says politics isn't broken. He is more idealistic today than he was yesterday. "But," he says, "the person I am is different to the one I was five and a half years ago. Not in terms of my values but in terms of my experience. I feel tested."

Several times, he uses his mother's death to answer a question. She is at the front of so much of his experience. When he says he feels tested, he hurries to clarify what he means: "My mum's died while I've been Leader of the Opposition."

He stops for a moment, then adds to this test the unions royal commission. "All sorts of crap thrown at me."

He describes the past five years as a series of stark episodes in which he is the constant. "I've seen off Tony Abbott and his crazy budget, his austere budget of cuts. Seen off the Malcolm Turnbull missed opportunity. You know, his premiership of the nation was one long missed opportunity. And now I contend with Morrison, who I think is taking Australia to a place in Australian politics we don't want to be."

He says optimism comes from knowing we can do better. He says the Labor Party is competitive. The phrase he uses is "competitive for purpose." He says the party's ideas are good ideas.

He is weighing himself in the conversation, finding the right voice. "This sense of potential is just fundamental," he says. "It tingles in me, what we can do."

*

On the phone from Melbourne, Scott Morrison is talking about the retirees' tax and the family business tax and the housing tax that he says will abolish negative gearing as we know it. He says the big kicker is that everyone will pay more income tax. He says bracket creep is a sneaky tax. He calls it obnoxious. The harder you work, the more you pay. The phrase he returns to is "as we know it." There is a now and it is certain and that is what he is promising.

It is Monday morning and he is talking to Alan Jones. They were at the races together on Saturday. The men trade figures. Jones says the numbers are confusing. He doesn't understand how Labor could be polling so well under Shorten. Morrison agrees: he doesn't know either.

"He can't manage money," Morrison says finally, "so he's coming after yours." And again: "This is what Labor does. They don't know how to manage money, so they come after yours with higher taxes. This is what we've always seen from Labor. This is fundamentally what this election is about: if you can't manage money, you can't run the country."

Morrison says that if you elect Labor you pay for a decade. He matches Jones's outrage, the rhythms of his rhetoric. His concern is for retirees. "The most offensive thing that Bill Shorten said yesterday was when he said that they don't pay tax. He said it was a 'gift.' A 'gift.' That's what he said to the retirees of Australia, and he said he was going to take that gift away from retirees right across this country."

Morrison calls tax a dead weight on the economy. He points again to Treasury figures that show Labor would collect $387 billion more in taxes over a decade. He says, "You saddle that on the economy." He says cafes will struggle. Rents will go up. "People's homes – the biggest thing that most Australians, you know, invest in, buy into, sweat for, to pay that mortgage off – the value of your own home is what will be under threat ... And even if you buy a new property, who are you going to sell it to? Thirty per cent of the market goes."

Morrison says one in five police officers have an investment property. He mentions his father's time as a cop. He mentions nurses and teachers who want to buy a flat rather than put their money in union-run super funds.

He lets Jones lead on the idea of death duties. No one is running this policy, but Morrison says it would be a disaster for the economy. He says it would be oblivion.

"This is an aspiration tax," he says. "They're going to tax people who are just working hard to try and get ahead. And, Alan, that's really what this election is about."

Jenny Morrison runs to get a pen. There is a group of children holding skateboards and they want her husband to sign them. The cameras are waiting. "Sharpie to the rescue," she says. Morrison says: "I never thought I'd be signing skateboards."

Both of them have a tendency to say out loud what they are doing. It is intended as reassurance but it can feel infantilising. He writes his name as "Scott." He signs six skateboards, a scooter and a helmet, and the arms of two children who have nothing else to be signed.

A little girl asks if he lives in a mansion. Another asks if it is a castle. "We come from the suburbs," Morrison says, "just like you guys do." A boy asks if he is rich. "Rich in life," he says, "because I've got a great family."

Morrison enjoys the attention. He lets his next appointment run half an hour late. The children's faces are pressed close together. They are jostling with each other to get nearer the prime minister. One of them is turning five and a press secretary tries in the background to get people singing "Happy Birthday." Jenny gives the boy a high five for each year he's been alive. There is nothing in today's schedule more important than these images. A boy asks the prime minister if he would like to try his skateboard. "I wish I could," Morrison says. "And I'm sure the cameras do, too."

People close to Morrison, the ones who like him, all say the same thing: "What you see is what you get." They intend it as an endorsement. They are conscious of his reputation for duplicity.

Morrison wants life to be simple. His Sundays are sacrosanct. He loves rugby league and his daughters' netball games. His faith is enormous. He sees virtue in long hours, the time of day being a marker of his diligence. He goads colleagues if the lights are out in their offices. He adores Tina Arena.

He loves the military and the police. Before he became treasurer, he would have liked the defence portfolio. He keeps a picture of his maternal grandfather in his office, in army uniform. There is a picture of the Queen near his desk and one of each of his daughters. A statue of two soldiers sits on the sideboard, the wounded one helped up on the other's back. On his bookshelf are spy novels, a few popular histories and Nam Le's collection *The Boat*. He says his favourite books are David Malouf's *The Great World* and Kate Grenville's *The Secret River*. He doesn't read international fiction. "I just don't relate to it. I'm interested in our stories."

When he acknowledges country, he thanks servicemen at the same time. The message is clear: this might be Indigenous land, but we fought for it. At his rallies, the Aboriginal flag is not on stage. He is close with former NSW police commissioner Andrew Scipione. His majors were economics and geography. His first job was at the property council and then in tourism. His preference is for the ordinary and the tangible.

*

Shorten is glib about where the election will be won. "In the ballot box," he says. "Everywhere."

He says Labor is competitive in jurisdictions and seats where it wouldn't normally hold out hope. He is hesitant to say where, but in the end he can't help himself. "We're looking at regional Queensland; Brisbane; north coast, south coast New South Wales; Sydney; Melbourne; Corangamite. I think Adelaide's got interesting again recently with the demise of Turnbull and Pyne. And, of course, Western Australia's the most interesting it's been in five or six electoral cycles. And I don't take northern Tassie for granted."

Shorten gets lost in his phone, looking at seats. He is absorbed by small details. He says there's a difference between now and 2016. The government is in chaos. The electorate has already given it the benefit of the doubt. "We got close in 2016 and one reason wasn't just our health-care campaign. They were inclined to give Turnbull a second chance on behalf of Abbott. I don't think Morrison goes to that same well of goodwill with the electorate. The CFA is not an issue the way it was in 2016. We're also more experienced. I don't know what football code you follow, but one thing you know about an AFL team that plays in its second grand final as opposed to the year before, if it was inexperienced, is you learn more. My team is now more experienced. Our policies are even more developed. So there's a whole range of factors … and of course, they've never explained why Malcolm Turnbull got dumped."

Shorten is on the way back to his office for a WeChat live-stream event with the Labor candidate for Chisholm, Jennifer Yang. The focus is Chinese voters. "It's pretty simple," a staffer says. "Last time, they beat us in the Chinese media."

*

On Tuesday, Labor takes down its negative gearing policy and replaces it with a factsheet. At a press conference in Bedford Park, Shorten becomes irritated with a question about the impact of his climate policy on the economy. "Let me just go to the record: I just said, four minutes ago, that Mr Morrison loves to boast about his strong economy. I'm pretty sure we were all here when I said that. But let me say it again, because I think it's a really good point to make. Mr Morrison loves to boast about his strong economy, but his strong economy is your classic Liberal strong economy. It's built upon two propositions. One, low wages. They're proud of it. They almost have a religious fervour, don't they, about being happy when the wages are low and corporate profits are up … And the second leg that he relies upon for this Liberal strong economy is the reduction, the reduction in real spending, on services."

Earlier, he stumbled on superannuation changes. He said there were none. He meant none beyond the ones he had already announced. He is having an unsteady first week. A close friend says the reason is personal. In Darwin, Shorten is irritated again. The anger is fresh in his eyes. A report has said Labor's climate policy will cost the country $25 billion. Shorten calls it a "baseless, fraudulent scare campaign of the Morrison government, backed up by their allies in some parts of the media." He says: "You know, these News Corp climate-change deniers and, of course, their ally the prime minister – a coal-wielding, climate-denying cave-dweller on this issue. You know, they all say, 'Look at the costs.' Well, they never mention the costs of the extreme weather events, do they? They never mention the cost of not getting into renewables. And they never mention energy prices, do they?"

He calls the debate "fundamentally dishonest." He says it is "malicious and stupid."

"In climate change, there will never be enough figures to satisfy the climate sceptics. If you don't believe in the science of climate change, no amount of evidence will ever convince you, because, fundamentally, it's a stupid position not to take action."

It is a basic tenet of politics that Oppositions don't win elections: governments lose them. Shorten is running like an incumbent, however. The Coalition is just waiting for him to fail.

*

Josh Frydenberg calls them new taxes. The figure he has is $387 billion over a decade, but $230 billion is Labor's rejection of tax cuts that have not been legislated. There is another $31 billion from changes to negative gearing and capital gains tax, and $57 billion from dividend imputations. The numbers were prepared by Treasury, but without instruction as to how the policies would interact. The department refused to offer a total figure.

"The total of Labor's new taxes is $387 billion over the decade," Frydenberg says, "taking tax as a share of the economy under Labor to 25.9 per cent, making a potential Shorten government the highest-taxing in Australian history."

Morrison's tax cuts depend on reducing spending. He denies this will mean cutting services. He says he is not cutting health or education. Analysis by the Grattan Institute shows he will need $40 billion a year in savings from 2030. The Coalition says this is realistic. It says jobs growth will reduce spending on welfare. The budget surplus it promises will mean less interest paid on debt.

Economists describe the assumptions as heroic. They mean stupid more than brave.

*

Morrison says he is uniquely prepared to lead the party. He tells people he has experience neither Turnbull nor Abbott could claim when they took the job. He says he has been in cabinet from day dot. He's been on the national security committee and the expenditure review committee. He says he succeeded in the Abbott government's first big test, stopping the boats.

People who know him say that once he believes something he will not change his mind. He does not like to answer questions. He has a willingness to lie or at least to serve his agenda before he knows the truth. Compensation is paid after he falsely accuses Save the Children staff of coaching refugees to harm themselves. When Reza Barati is beaten to death inside the Manus Island detention centre, Morrison wrongly claims he had been outside the fence. "If people are going to seek to disrupt the centres … they will put themselves at risk if they go beyond that perimeter fence and I don't think that is behaviour that should be encouraged."

Confronted over his Save the Children comments, he says: "I drew no conclusions on the material that had been presented to me at the time." And: "I did the job that I had to do in that situation."

Often he will say he is expressing a view he has heard, or acting on the sentiments of others. He separates himself from the job. He is a conduit for the nation as a priest is for god. Morrison says he is practical. Others call him transactional. He gets things done. His nickname, at one point, was Rottweiler.

When in shadow cabinet he raises the possibility of exploiting the fear of Muslims, he says he is doing so to make sure it doesn't happen. He asks at times for his actions to mean their opposite. He says he has private reckonings, that he is not on Oprah's couch.

Morrison governs in his own image. He struggles to imagine experiences that are not his. He says anti-gay conversion therapy is not an issue for him. He says he won't send his children to public schools because he doesn't like the morals taught in them. He is the first prime minister to make such a distinction. He speaks "as a parent." On complex issues, he forms a quorum: "Jenny and I."

"In the past I've been criticised, I've been mocked, I've been attacked," he says. "People say, 'That will never work' and 'This will never work' and 'You're wrong' and all this. And then it works. And I was right. And that's the approach I will continue to take."

Shorten loves cards because he loves to win. Occasionally, he plays his staff. He recalls the last game and at the memory of it throws both hands in the air like a boxer. He is standing in the middle of a shopping mall. "I won," he says. "I was the champion."

The wings of his jacket open out and his pants hang a little. Pleasure lights on his face. "I love all sorts of card games," he says. "I love 500. I let my bridge go, but I was good at bridge for a while."

Morrison's love is rugby: first union, now league. He is the Sharks' No. 1 ticket holder. When he was younger, he was a front-row forward. He is a great barracker. Sometimes, he will finish press conferences by saying "Go Sharkies." He gives locker-room nicknames to his colleagues. He calls them Birmo and Hirsty and Big Mac and The Kunk.

Shorten considers the degree to which he is always a cardplayer, how much he relishes the strategy. His voice becomes quiet. "I think there's some manifestations of my card playing which reflect my more general persona. That's quite perceptive. I'm a bid hog. I love winning the bid in 500. It's bad. I'm naughty. I love a win. And I always do try and watch every card that gets played. And I love finessing. But I do not think 500 is life. I just think it's a game."

Shorten can't leave the factions alone. He can't give it up. Senior figures say it has hurt him. Hawke stepped back from the numbers once he was leader. Others say Shorten has done something only Whitlam achieved: he has stopped the fighting. He knows who to pay and how to pay them.

Shorten says that if he wins there will be less butcher's paper than in the last Labor parliament. He has learnt from that period. A senior figure says he is good. He puts it like this: "Rudd was an utter cunt. Julia was fine but she wasn't good – and good's enough in politics."

*

In his first speech as prime minister, Scott Morrison looks to Menzies. He is in Albury, where the modern Liberal Party was founded. He says he is there to pledge. He says he likes ritual.

He speaks to Menzies' conception of the individual: "It's all about the individual, and the capacity and the value and sanctity." He speaks to the family as the foundation of society. Then to community. He speaks to home ownership. He speaks to freedom of religion and of speech. He speaks to stable jobs. He looks into the past and it affirms his present. "In coming here today, a new generation of Liberal leaders are embracing all of those beliefs," he says. "They remain as relevant today as when he first said them."

He has a quote written on a piece of paper, a line of Menzies' from 1943: "No party seizes the imagination of the people unless the people know the party stands for certain things, and we'll fight for those things until the bell rings."

Morrison says he believes in effort. People will be rewarded but only if they try. It is similar to his notion of faith: God has blessings to give and they come to those who are worthy. "I think that's what fairness means in this country," he says. "It's not about everybody getting the same thing. If you put in, you get to take out, and you get to keep more of what you earn."

He talks about making a contribution. He says he doesn't believe people should be taxed to improve the lives of others. He says that's not how it works. He says he wants an Australia based on values. He knows people are doing it tough. He talks about the sweat of hard work. He talks about the power of prayer. He talks about the dignity of retirees. "I'll finish where I started – I'll finish where Menzies started," he says. "It all starts with the individual."

He doesn't yet have a name for these people. He knows just that they are out there and their desires are decent. They want the best for themselves and that is the best for the country. He knows these people feel overlooked and when he pledges he is pledging to them.

*

The Liberals are grateful to Tim Wilson. The parliamentary inquiry he holds into franking credits has given a human face to those affected by Labor's policy. The day after Morrison becomes leader, Wilson calls up to pitch the idea. He sets up a petition website at the same time as he is chairing the inquiry, calling the reform a "retirement tax." He takes evidence from a relative without disclosing their relationship. Liberal Party lobbyists front the hearings without saying that's what they are. Wilson writes a form letter, which is then lodged among complaints.

Retirees say they will stop giving to charity. They warn of cuts: "Our gardener and cleaner will have to go." One man giving evidence says that "to target a minority group like this is wrong." A woman says, "we will not become stolen-from generation without a fight."

Internally, people are telling Shorten to stop saying "the top end of town." They say: "You're insulting them, and then you're taking their money."

Labor's reforms affect about five in every hundred people, the majority of them wealthy. But the issue is perfect for the Coalition. Six times that number say they are worried about it. Wilson says: "In the same way that kids told their parents how to vote in the marriage equality postal survey, we saw parents tell their kids about the cost of voting Labor."

*

Shorten says "fuck" when he wants to press on you his friendship. Or worse, when he does not want you to write down the thing he's saying. It's a politician's trick: instead of taking a conversation off the record, you fill it with intimacies and hope the journalist will settle for them in place of quotes.

"What?" he says. "It's just more fucking – if it's anything from Jane Cadzow's piece, you should just put it in the bin."

The question is about his brother's popularity at school, how he succeeded at sport, was taller and more handsome. Shorten is reaching for jocularity. After thirty minutes, the interview has settled and is comfortable.

"No," he says. "No, I'm not going to ... No, it's not that I'm not interested ... The amount of time I give thinking to my secondary school years, and particular triumphs or otherwise, is very small."

The Cadzow piece came out four years earlier. It mentioned his brother only briefly. It pictured Shorten as ruthless and assured. It doubted his authenticity. It mentioned his wit and charisma and how these things fail to accompany him onto television.

A former colleague said Shorten was pretending to make ratatouille on *Kitchen Cabinet*. "He puts his arm around Chloe, he kisses her on the cheek. This is all role-playing. You don't see the real person."

The piece said Shorten was estranged from his father. It said how Richard Pratt had filled that role. It quoted his stepmother saying she hadn't seen him since the funeral. "He and I were supposed to be co-executors of his father's will, but he just didn't respond any time I tried to call him," she said. "I had a few personal things of his father's that I thought might have been of interest to him in the event that he eventually had some children, but I'm still holding them here."

At one point, an adviser reads to Shorten a quote from Greg Hunt criticising Labor's climate policy. Shorten sighs and says, so Cadzow can hear: "God, they tell fucking lies."

The article ends with an assessment from Earl Setches, a factional ally of Shorten's. He says Bill has "Phar Lap's heart beating in the body of an aardvark."

*

Barnaby Joyce didn't look into the vendor. He doesn't know why the valuation was so high. The Labor Party had bought from the same people. He says it was a fair price. His voice is worn thin by exasperation.

The story is about water bought from a company linked to energy minister Angus Taylor, domiciled in the Cayman Islands. The deal was worth $80 million.

"I've got no idea," Joyce says. "If there was cheaper water out there, they would have bought it. We have got people who are paid a hell of a lot of money to go out and determine that and then they refer that back to the minister. I do not go out and purchase the water. I do not even determine the vendor. I do not determine the price."

He rants. He says Labor, Labor, Labor, Labor. Then, suddenly, his mood shifts. "Cut to the chase," he says. "You're saying, 'Is Angus Taylor somehow tied up with this?' Be straight, mate. Say what you mean. Spit it out. No, don't duck and weave. Be straight ... Come on, spit it out."

The noise around what he is saying drops out. The words become very precise. "I never knew Angus Taylor. I wouldn't have known him if he stood up in my cornflakes, before he came into parliament."

In any ordinary campaign, this would be a big story. It would cost votes.

*

Shorten has an extraordinary need to be liked. He cares hugely. He calls ahead of journalists. He once had his stepdaughter's schoolteacher speak to a reporter to confirm he was on the phone with her the night he was photographed doing numbers against Kevin Rudd. At his mother's funeral he is pleased to see his old piano teacher. He asks her if he was a better student than his brother. He is happy enough with the answer to retell the story.

Privately, he doubts the preferred prime minister figure. He tells people it is the most bullshit poll ever invented. He tells himself that people think they are being asked, Who is the prime minister?

"I feel popular every day, mate," he says. "I feel popular every day. You should've come with me to the TAFE this morning, hundreds of people I'd never met before. They loved me. So that bloke, down on his luck over there, wanted to have a chat with me. I'd never met him before. Half a dozen voters walked by, nodded and smiled. It doesn't worry me. Like, when people get to see me being positive as well as oppositionalist, I think we'll do well. And remember: Turnbull was more popular than me; Abbott was more popular initially. How did that work out?"

Shorten squints, as if checking the size of what he's about to say. His eyelashes are uncommonly long. He has the large, pleading eyes of a child left alone in his cot. It is one of the qualities that make people uncertain about him: need.

Has he thought about who Scott Morrison is, what defines him? "A little bit, yeah."

There's a pause, not to decide what he will say but to invest it with humility. "I find him a bit hard to interpret. I know his Christianity – his Pentecostalism – is very important to him, so – I don't know how much that is him. I find him hard to – Is this for after the election?"

It is.

"I don't know who the real Scott Morrison is sometimes ... Is he far-right wing? Is he not? I don't know. I don't know."

*

Morrison lets the cameras in for one song. He puts his hand into the air and lets it wash over him. The lights tint his shirt a misty lavender. His face goes cerise. It is Easter Sunday and the Horizon Church is full. His eyes close as he sings. "It's a message of humility," he says. "It's a message of love for each other, of selflessness; it's a message of putting others before yourself and that's what this community does and that's why it's as strong as it is." He says the Pentecostal faith is a community of love. He says it has been a tremendous support to him personally. "This has been the bedrock of our family. They're a wonderful community and they reach out all across the community, they always have."

God gives Morrison's politics its certainty. He worships in a congregation where the people are each very similar. On the difficult issues, he speaks of prayer. When he is imploring, he says that the people will light him. "I will burn for you every day. Every single day."

Shorten is edgy about his faith. He spends Easter Sunday in Brisbane with his family. He attends an Anglican service. Shorten says he worships "intermittently." And then, to be certain: "very intermittently." He calls his faith "Catholic and Christian in background." Pushed for detail, he says: "Not dogmatic. There's elements of the faith which have more meaning to me than other parts. Less into the ceremony and less into the symbolism. The idea that everyone is born equal? Everyone has a soul? I get that. That drives my view of people. I think everyone's equal; not necessarily 'we're all equally good at things,' but there's something good in nearly everyone."

He is reluctant to say whether he believes there is a god. "I don't feel I have an invisible friend giving me invisible advice on a daily basis. But I do believe in my social justice teachings I learnt," he says. "I think that a person's goodness or merit is not measured by their wealth or their skin colour or their gender, where they live, how many houses they have." He stops again, reframes: "It's how you treat people. You know, the golden rule: treat people the way you'd like to be treated."

Before the campaign, Morrison draws a road map of winnable seats. He marks Lindsay in western Sydney. He marks Dobell on the NSW central coast, although colleagues doubt him. He feels positive about Queensland, and sees a few opportunities in Victoria and Western Australia. He campaigns on this road map, seat by seat. The party calls it "guerilla warfare."

Morrison has a gift for strategy. He revels in the complexity of it. At key times in his life, it has gone very wrong. Other times, it has gone exactly right.

He has conceived of a voter he will eventually call the Quiet Australian. They are Menzies' Forgotten People, the middle class who risk being ground between the millstones of the rich and the poor. "The middle class who, properly regarded, represent the backbone of this country."

Morrison tracks twenty seats closely. His concern is for home owners and retirees. He says these people are humble and decent. They shouldn't be punished for looking after themselves. He says Shorten sneers at them. Focus groups show up worry at the cost of Labor's agenda. Morrison says negative gearing changes will destroy the property market, where these people have their money. He says Labor's changes to dividend imputations will be a tax on retirement. The messages test well and he sticks to them.

*

Shorten says he remembers a little bit of kindergarten but not much. He says *Robin Hood* was the first book he really liked, but he doesn't remember when he read it. He remembers that when he was a child his family took only three holidays. He remembers the day he got sunburnt on South Melbourne Beach.

"We had three holidays," he says. "Mum was working. Dad wasn't – Dad was born in 1929. I think he had a pretty rough life in the Depression, which meant that he didn't necessarily have a lot of memories to draw on to be a father."

He complained to his mother that she didn't volunteer in the tuckshop at the Jesuit school he attended. He complained that she didn't dress up like the other mothers. These two memories are vivid and unprompted, sustained all this time by the sense of not fitting in. He remembers being confronted by the wealth of the kids he went to school with. The great embarrassment of this time came at his graduation dinner. His father fell asleep at the table, drunk.

In Shorten's office is a copy of Ramsina Lee's book *Workers' Inferno*, about the explosion at the Esso gas plant in Longford. Gillian Triggs's book is there, under some papers. There is a "Make Moonee Ponds Great Again" hat and a framed honorary membership from the Showmens Guild of Australia. On the top shelf, Bob Ellis's *And So It Went* still has a place. There is a cartoon of a noose and another of a lynching. There is Roy Masters' book *Bad Boys*, about misconduct in sport, and Peter FitzSimons' biography of labour-hire don Frank Hargrave. On the wall is a painting of a shearer, his blade held up to the sheep's neck. Shorten likes to tell staffers how odd it is that in paintings such as this the men are never sweating.

*

As a child, Scott Morrison was in church productions with his family. In *Oliver!* he played the Artful Dodger. His father played Fagin. Shorten was in a composite Gilbert and Sullivan in Grade 6. He was in the chorus, as a fairy. His brother was a pirate.

"I remember it, I think, because I didn't really like it," Shorten says. "I suspect that I wanted a better role, but I also knew I couldn't sing. So if you like it was where hope – It's where aspiration met reality and reality won."

An agent saw Morrison in a church production and signed him for work in television commercials. He was in one for Hungry Jack's and another for AMP and one for Vicks cough drops. "I was: 'Vicks will lick a tickling throat,'" he says, remembering the jingle. "Well, they stick in your head, don't they?"

At some point in the past three years, Shorten stopped telling jokes. He says maybe it's just that the jokes are funnier, so you don't notice them as much. He won't say who told him to stop.

"It's a particular art form," he says. "You know, there's Indonesian puppet performance, there's kabuki and then there's press conferences. I reckon Indonesian puppets and kabuki are easier to master than press conferences. They've got more theme, more art to them. So, yeah, it's taken me a while to get that … and I haven't got it right. Yeah."

Staffers call it "the zinger phase." They say, "We got through the zinger phase."

*

Before the election, Shorten declines to meet with Rupert Murdoch. He gets a call for a sitdown in New York but he doesn't take it. He is the first contemporary leader to do so.

The *Daily Telegraph*'s first front page in the campaign reads "Tax Time Bomb." It claims to reveal Labor's $387 billion blowout. "Bill Shorten would lead the highest-taxing government in Australia's history," it says, "with his policies amounting to a $387 billion tax hit on families and the economy over the next decade."

The newspaper runs a scare campaign against electric cars. It runs slurs against Zali Steggall. It runs a beat-up on students and climate activism, under the headline "Kiddie Pawn." It says Shorten's campaign is short-circuiting. Every policy is a raid. On Anzac Day, it warns of "a raft of radical Labor policies on transgender issues will result in children undergoing unnecessary sex change procedures."

It warns of Labor voters as trendy and affluent. Again on page one, it runs the Coalition's "hit list" of cars Shorten's climate policies will apparently ban. The next day it calls child-care funding and dental subsidies a "sweetheart deal." It says: "Labor 'raids' rich in tax and spend gamble." On bulk-billing for pathology tests, it runs the headline "Blood Money." When Morrison makes an announcement on energy prices, the front-page headline is "ScoMo's Bill Attack: 25% power pledge to energise campaign." Then it's "ScoMo's Home Run: ALP scrambles to match PM's house plan." In a special report, they label Shorten "The Great Divider." The subheading reads: "Who will win and lose in Shorten's class war."

*

Shorten takes a piece of paper and draws a family tree. It is stubby and incomplete, growing into the top left corner of the page. There are no marriages on it, only individuals. He starts with his father. He writes "Bill S." He draws a line up from there to his grandmother, Betty. He says she was a strong lady. He draws a line up from her, and starts to write "Bill" again. He crosses it out and writes "William Menzies Cameron." "He was born in 1880," Shorten says, tracing the line down. "She was born about 1906. He was born in 1929. Then there's me: I was born in 1967."

Unprompted, he says, "I got a lot of history in me." He says his great-grandfather was a Labour councillor in Britain, one of the Jarrow Marchers. He says his grandmother was a barmaid and cleaner. She lived in a council house. On both sides, Shorten is one generation from poverty. He was raised in the afterimage of that anxiety. Recently he spoke to a cousin who told him his grandmother would have been proud of him. The statement thrills him, even in recollection.

"When people say, 'Ah, yeah. Bill's one thing in the boardroom or another thing in the factory,' they don't realise my background," he says. "It's in the constant struggle for fair treatment of people." He points to his great-grandfather: "That's what he did." And to his grandmother: "That's how she lived her life." And to his dad: "He's a bit more of a good-time guy."

Shorten says his father was larger than life. He says it with the weariness of someone who knows what the euphemism really means. He is bristling a little. He doesn't know if he wants to talk about this. "My dad wasn't a good father," he says eventually. "And he drank, far too much. And the marriage with Mum broke down eventually."

There is tenderness in what he is saying, and reckoning. "He wasn't a bad man. But what is interesting: I mean, a lot of who we are as adults is written for us by our parents when we're children. So he didn't have role models, because his father died. Being raised by a single mum during World War II, not straightforward. Not straightforward. No money. So in many ways he was raised by his grandfather."

Shorten works hard to make it seem as if the observations are about his father's upbringing.

Property records show Peter Dutton sold his Canberra unit in February. It was listed as "near new" with a "peaceful heritage outlook." The agent promised "the best of both worlds." In sales pictures, a stack of books includes Jonathan Darman's *Landslide*. It is the story of how Lyndon Johnson and Ronald Reagan tried to remake America in the wake of the Kennedy assassination, ending consensus politics. A spokesperson says Dutton has bought another unit off the plan. Dutton says he intends to serve a full term. "Without any doubt," he says.

*

Shorten talks about his opponents in terms of what sustains them, the trait from which they draw their purpose. Each of them he can reduce to a single energy. "Abbott from his ideology," he says. "Maybe Turnbull from his patrician nature, his sense of noblesse oblige. Morrison maybe from his faith."

He considers Morrison a moment longer. "He has a huge self-confidence," he says. "I don't know if he's prone to introspection or not. Every sentence is uttered with a sort of bellicosity. Not bellicosity: he seems to … I just wonder if his faith gives him that confidence, the sense that he's chosen. I don't know. I don't really want to talk too negatively about him."

Shorten talks a lot about confidence, especially self-confidence. His answer about his own drive is unconvincing: that he is driven by his policies, that he knows what he can do for the country. In his mind, he is an outsider. He has always sought mentors: Robert Ray early on, Bill Kelty more consistently.

"They all exude a level of self-confidence," he says of his opponents. "I don't think they're introspective about … They don't seem to suffer from self-doubt. Maybe that's a presentation."

Shorten is weary of ease. He resents certainty in others. He is not tall and his suits are not well cut. He is handsome but not attractive. He finds television difficult. In photographs, he prefers not to take off his jacket.

"I don't know about doubt, but I don't take anything for granted," he says. "I don't think I know it all."

*

Approval for Adani's groundwater plan is given before the country's lead science agencies have seen it. It is the last federal clearance needed for the project. The CSIRO and Geoscience Australia are given a verbal briefing, and on the basis of their responses Melissa Price approves the mine.

The day before, Matt Canavan visits the prime minister. He denies threatening to resign if the mine is not approved. He has a tweet he plans to send out if the Coalition wins: Start Adani.

The CSIRO response warns that "there are still components of that advice that will need to be addressed." Earlier correspondence from the two agencies says the data on which Adani is depending is unverified and that the approaches proposed do "not comprehensively address the uncertainty" regarding contamination.

In her press release, Price says both agencies have independently assessed the mine's revised plans. The following day, she approves the Yeelirrie uranium mine in Western Australia. The Supreme Court is still waiting to rule on the legality of its state approvals.

*

Morrison's career is marked by plotting. As a tourism executive, he undermined his rivals. He would create vast, intricate schemes to get ahead. His own party does not know what faction he sits in. He has a knack for accidents and he made his leadership look like one.

Even when it is over, it isn't. He lost his first preselection with only eight votes, then came back and took the seat from the successful candidate.

*

Shorten's advisers are pushing preferencing stories. They share a story from the *Morning Bulletin* in Rockhampton and another about One Nation's candidate in the Hunter, who doubts what happened at Port Arthur and in the 9/11 terrorist attacks. "*The Australian* reports this morning that the Nationals will put this person above Labor in its preferences."

Campaign staff concede they lost television in the first two weeks. The focus on health policy is an issue. "Every shot we gave them was someone getting chemo."

Shorten's response is curious: more hospital press conferences. In this election he is betting against modern politics. His policy announcements go for an hour. At press conferences, he will take forty-five minutes of questions. Morrison will do ten minutes, if he takes questions at all. A solitary camera captures Shorten's speeches in full. It drifts in and out of focus. When a protester invades the stage, the footage is put online unedited. Shorten avoids streetwalks and doesn't do manufactured picture opportunities. "Morrison is better every day," a television journalist says. "Every single day. I mean, he's shearing a fucking sheep."

Shorten's gamble is that you can replace popularity with policy. If he is right, he upends decades of political orthodoxy. If he is wrong, this may be the last policy election for a generation. The press travelling with Shorten see him winning, despite it. "Everything would have to go right for Morrison. And then he's still got to get kissed on the dick."

*

Linda Burney is standing at the front of the room. Pat Dodson stands off to one side. Mark Dreyfus is on his haunches, talking to an elderly couple seated near the back. The man turns his head and it's Bill Kelty.

The lift is too small. It brings people up in clutches. Shorten arrives to a standing ovation. The announcement is long and multifaceted, giving new money and support to women affected by family violence. Shorten speaks with confidence about the policy package. He finds moments of softness. The room seats about 150 people and is the right size for him.

He talks about the smallness, the meanness, the narrowness of the Coalition. "How did we come to a state in Australian politics where the government of the day says we have nothing new to offer you but we want you to be afraid: afraid of change, afraid of reform, afraid of the future? Afraid of the march of women towards equality. Afraid of every new idea, every big challenge … They find an excuse to do nothing every time."

He says when the Coalition say we can't afford something, they mean we don't deserve it. He talks about a vision to write Australia large. He refers to those in the room as friends. He finishes by talking about his mother. He says she was a feminist before the word existed. He says she was a brilliant woman, but she was denied opportunities. She took a teaching scholarship because she couldn't afford to study law.

"She was never bitter because of what happened to her. But she always felt because of her family's financial circumstances, because of the era she grew up in, and because she was a woman, it was never assumed that she should have the same opportunity to fulfil her potential, to decide her own future. That if she had been the eldest son – with the best will in the world to my grandparents – if she had been the eldest son I suspect she wouldn't have had to take the teaching scholarship."

Shorten bends his arms at the elbows and sets his fingertips together like a gate. It is as if he is circumscribing a plot of land in front of him and then explaining how he plans to tend it. He says if people are denied opportunity because of race or class or gender, the country misses out on their contribution. "If we can achieve true equality for the women of Australia," he says, "then this will be the fairest and the richest nation in the world." He says, "There's one more step we need to take. So, let's get out there and win this election. Let's turn words into actions."

There is a second standing ovation. Kelty is last to his feet. He doesn't clap. "He did good today," he says as the room empties. "He spoke in stories."

*

Clive Palmer says Anthony Chisholm, the Queensland Labor senator, called to see if they could do a deal. "He called me on Wednesday when he was with Bill Shorten in central Queensland and he said, was it too late to do preferences? It's not true that I wasn't approached by the ALP."

Later, Palmer says he changed his mind. "I then turned on the television," he says, "and Bill Shorten was saying a lot of things about me which were untrue. He was lying to the Australian people. And I then decided I want nothing further to do with him or his party because they were two-faced liars. The language he used was not fit for consumption by our children and I realised he was unfit to be prime minister of Australia."

Morrison is blunt about what he needs from Palmer: "I'm interested in forming a government on the other side of this election. I'm going to make sure I do everything I possibly can to ensure that we're able to form that government."

Morrison says Shorten is seeking a "coronation." He says he sees the election as a "rubber-stamp." It's a refinement of an earlier line: "What I know is Bill Shorten, he has already measured up the curtains and for all I know he has probably gone out and bought the curtains, but my suggestion is he should keep the receipt."

It's a good line. It plays into the same sense of entitlement that made Shorten a faceless man. It's a way of talking about leadership without Morrison mentioning his own.

*

At his women's speech, Shorten talks about the threat of a drunk father. He talks about a man who falls asleep at the table. This is not in his prepared remarks. He leaves off on a line that has been written for him, about words not putting a roof over someone's head. He talks about the unknowing, the instability experienced by the children of alcoholics. These children are never settled.

"Words don't help kids coming home at night, checking if their mother has turned on the light on the porch, or not, as a quiet sign to say whether the dad is in a good mood or an angry mood," he says. "Words don't help kids in the morning and their mothers wondering, where would they go? How much longer can they take it? Words don't help children at night, or their mother, trying to negotiate the unpredictable moods of an angry man. Is he drunk-happy or is he drunk-angry? Will he fall asleep at the table? Can I turn my music on in my room? Will it cause a fight? Does my mother have to physically and literally protect me from the moods of the angry man?"

In the front row, his wife, Chloe, cries.

*

At a press conference in Townsville, Morrison puts his arm around his candidate. Phil Thompson served in Afghanistan. He struggled with alcohol after stepping on a bomb. His memory was lost. Moments before facing the cameras, he was told a friend he served with has committed suicide.

"That's why I had my arm on him during the press conference. I don't usually do that," Morrison says. "The really sad thing for me was that he didn't look surprised."

*

Palmer holds his hand in the air. "I've got four thousand million dollars. I've got five hundred million dollars in the bank today."

His face is on every spare billboard in the country. He has full-page ads in every newspaper and spots on every television network. Almost all of them attack Labor. He is spending more on advertising in this campaign than the other parties combined. The figure is upwards of $60 million.

Palmer has no policies. His intentions are grandiose and empty. He is already naming ministers for his Potemkin cabinet. Still, his preferences could deliver the Liberals at least two seats. His hope is to open up his coalmine in the Galilee Basin, alongside Adani's.

Privately, senior figures in the Coalition worry that he is debasing political advertising. They worry that he has spent so much, on so lurid an approach, that when they go to spend in the final weeks people will have already turned off.

The sky in Tasmania is low and grey and looks like a pot scourer. Shorten is here to announce a tourism package, including $50 million for the expansion of MONA. Party operatives are worried the money will upset marginals in the state's north. The bus moves through the outer suburbs of Hobart. A dolls' house goes by on the back of a trailer. A man walks his German shepherd, bald except for his headphones.

David Walsh meets Shorten in a t-shirt that reads, "Sell your soul." This will be the first significant government investment in MONA. "I suppose I'll be told I'm taking money out of hospitals or geriatric care," Walsh says.

The television cameras cannot adjust to the light in the James Turrell work *Beside Myself*. A cameraman warns his colleagues not to look through their viewfinders. "You'll fall over, mate." The photographers ask if Shorten and Anthony Albanese can walk through again. On the first try, they were only silhouettes. "You don't want Julie Collins?" a staffer asks. "It is her electorate."

At the press conference, Shorten asks what assurances have been given to Clive Palmer by the Coalition. He asks whether gun laws will be relaxed or Palmer's debt forgiven. He steps to one side and lets Albanese add to the answer. He smiles as Albanese outperforms him. He did the same with Penny Wong the day before. He seems happy there are people in his party better at this than him.

"Scott Morrison had a choice," Albanese says, "between standing up for ripped-off workers or sucking up to a tosser who ripped them off. And he chose the tosser. He chose Clive Palmer."

*

Shorten wears a Brooks Brothers jacket. His chinos are worn at the hem. He enters Salamanca Market like a predator scanning for small fish. His head moves this way and that. His hand darts out. He says the same thing to everyone he encounters. "How do you do? Bill Shorten. Nice to see you."

Sometimes, each part will be directed at a different person. He doesn't wait for an answer to the first question, but pauses if they speak after the last phrase. "How do you do? Bill Shorten. Nice to see you."

The press pack is in front of him. This is only his second streetwalk of the campaign. The last was in Adelaide. He ate an oyster. "I just need a little bit more room, guys," he says. "Otherwise I'll never meet another human being."

A woman says she would rather die than be in a picture with him. Another says she doubts he even likes the curry he is buying. He has a wad of small notes loose in his pocket. He puts five dollars into the box of a small boy busking. A cameraman asks if he will eat an oyster. A minder responds with a slow, deep nod. So much of politics can feel like an in-joke.

"Have you got a small one?" he asks at the oyster stall. "Buffet. Thanks." He chews the oyster and grimaces slightly. "Stunning."

Peter Barron is watching. He stands back on the grass like the driver at a mafia funeral. The next day, he positions himself in a doorframe on the edge of Shorten's rally. His suit is black and boxy. His hair has thinned to nothing. He walks from his shoulders down, the way a pendulum swings in a clock. Barron is a fixture of the NSW Right, a former adviser to Neville Wran and Bob Hawke. He is there every day of Shorten's campaign. He has the tight, dangerous smile of an old man who knows things.

*

In the video they are making for the Coalition launch, Jenny Morrison says her husband used to buy her flowers but then he stopped. She says the day he proposed was unromantic. They were sitting on a bench at the top of Martin Place when he asked. She laughed at him: she didn't think it was serious.

The music shifts and they are talking about IVF. "I desperately wanted to be a parent, but I didn't want it to destroy our lives together," Morrison says to the camera. "At some point you have to imagine your life without having kids, and that's a very painful thing to do."

Morrison calls their first daughter a miracle. He calls their second daughter a blessing. There is a sense with Morrison's family that he is not so much using them to campaign: he is retreating into them.

*

The room has a disco ball and an echo. A blowfly hum comes through the sound system. The Demi Lovato song "Confident" is playing. Over and over, the chorus asks: "What's wrong with being, What's wrong with being, What's wrong with being confident?"

Young men with nervous legs walk backwards and forwards or rattle in place. They are not sure if they should take off their hats. Young women in Labor sweatshirts help volunteers to their seats. The song plays on, each verse more precocious: "I used to hold my freak back, Now I'm letting go, I make my own choice, Bitch, I run this show, So leave the lights on, No, you can't make me behave."

The rally is at Box Hill Town Hall. There is sense of civic optimism about the building's white columns and wood panelling. Beds of pansies are planted out, the flowers a handspan from one another. Inside, the stage is washed red. A Punch and Judy curtain is drawn halfway closed. Shorten's staff are excited about the announcement. "It's a good old-fashioned campaign day."

The doors close and the music stops. A screen plays clips of Tony Abbott saying there will be no cuts to education and Joe Hockey smoking a cigar with Mathias Cormann. There is a clip of Ged Kearney winning the Batman by-election. There are signs that read "Vote for Medicare" and "Vote for jobs" and "Vote for education" and "Vote for women's rights" and "Vote for our planet."

Shorten is introduced as "the next prime minister of Australia." It takes a full two minutes for him to walk from the back of the room to the stage. He puts his hands in the air and claps with the rest of the crowd. The smile on his face is not an easy one. It is straight and cautious. As the cheer continues it opens and becomes comfortable.

A boy rushes the stage. He has a sign that says, "Don't frack our future." He drops the sign before anyone can read it and is pulled from the stage before he can get off the jumper that is covering his "Stop Adani" t-shirt. The boy yells "Climate emergency." Shorten smiles and looks straight ahead. He makes the same face he makes at press conferences. "And you know what?" he says, stirring the air in front of him with a finger. "Those people who want action on climate change: don't protest against Labor; vote the government out."

He says there is a foundational difference between him and Morrison. "It is fundamentally two different views of leadership, him and I. He thinks it's all about him, and I'm proud to lead a united, talented team."

Shorten genuinely likes Wong. He has built a friendship with Tanya Plibersek. He doesn't like Albanese, but everybody knows that. He works well with him and has guaranteed him a seat in cabinet. He is good at listening. He respects his team and they respect him.

Shorten collects model battlefields. Before the election, his reading is in what he calls "a real Roman history phase." The book in his travel bag is Adam Zamoyski's *Napoleon: The man behind the myth.*

*

The signs behind Scott Morrison say, "Lower taxes" and "A stronger economy" and "Secure borders." He speaks with a microphone in his hand. "So, friends," he says, "there's a lot at stake. There's a lot at stake." He has the preacher's trick of repeating himself, and then speaking quickly to emphasis the urgency of his mission. "And I want to thank you for being here on a Sunday. And being here to support us here today. You know what's at stake. This is the best country in the world to live."

He walks across the stage. He has a small table with three glasses of water on it and a large Australian flag strung up behind him. "The road ahead depends on managing the economy and managing money," he says, "because as John Howard said, if you can't manage money, as Labor can't, you can't run the country. And our future depends on building our economy to secure your future. Thank you very much."

He talks about setting up the country for success. He says people matter. His announcement is money for congestion and a cap on the refugee intake. He is in Homebush, where the two issues have been erroneously linked before. "If you believe in immigration being a key part of Australia's future, which I do, and my party does, then you have to make sure you have an immigration program which is sustainable, which has integrity, which focuses on people being able to come and get jobs and become part of the community," he says. "That is the overwhelming story of the Australian immigration experience. Run it too hot, you put that all at risk."

He says, "We've got our borders and the budget under control. We make decisions about who comes here based on what's in Australia's interests."

John Howard speaks at the same rally. His tie runs past his belt buckle and his hand seems to be gripping a newel post that isn't there. He says the politics of division has emerged for the first time in a long time. "Bill Shorten thought this campaign was going to be a coronation," he says. "He thought all he'd have to do was wave with one hand and get through a few set-piece presentations ... and he would have a very easy victory. But something has happened along the way ... and people started asking questions."

*

Shorten's tie is pulled off to one side. He can be several people in the course of a half-hour speech. His confidence comes and then leaves him. It moves across his face and settles in his eyes. It makes his voice uneven. At times, he speaks as if he's giving participation prizes at a dance eisteddfod. The stage lighting doesn't help. Other times, he seems as if he is reading a storybook to children. His emphasis is there to make outsized moral points. Occasionally, though, his confidence holds and what it is he's saying lines up with the way in which he's saying it. In these moments, he is a skilled politician.

He announces what he calls "a new policy push." He says there will be a huge revamp of subsidies for dental care. It will affect three million pensioners and older people. He calls it "the fair go in action." He sees an old friend in the audience. The friend is already in Shorten's prepared remarks. The notes read: "I can see a friend of mine in the audience today, Gary ... mate, I know your diagnosis isn't good ... the fact that you're here means the world to me ... And you are why we're fighting for this."

He calls this announcement a "dividend of our tax reforms." He links it to inequality. He uses his storybook voice to admonish the top end of town. "We believe subsidising dental care for three million Aussie pensioners and seniors is more important than protecting tax loopholes for millionaires."

He talks about imbalance and unfairness and rich people with "the luxury of a whole lot of deductions and perks and accounting tricks." He makes another announcement: $4 billion for universal preschool and salary rises to childcare workers.

"Today, I am proud to announce the most family-friendly policy of this campaign," he says, "and the biggest saving for family budgets in a generation."

There are hungry cheers. The small, dark hall in Box Hill has the feeling of excitement in it. Shorten says they need to make the election about their plans for the future. "No fake news or lies on social media, no poisonous slogans from the advertising agency masquerading as the Liberal government will deter us from making the case."

He moves slow through the crowd. The song has finished before he can reach the back of the room. The second-last hand he shakes is Miranda Devine's. The News Corp columnist is seated in the back row. As Shorten leaves, a television reporter checks through the announcement with a staffer, counting each point on his thumb. "A thousand bucks. Every two years. Age pensioners."

Peter Dutton's wife does an interview with the *Sunday Mail*. The page-one headline reads: "My Pete's No Monster." The piece says their family has been the subject of death threats and "demented" abuse. It says she "spoke of her husband's private persona in a bid to show another side of one of Australia's most hard-nosed politicians." It quotes her saying: "He is really a good man. He is really a good father, and he's not a monster."

*

The first Newspoll of the campaign is 49–51. It is the best result since Morrison took office. Still, the Coalition would lose between six and ten seats, even with preferences from Palmer and One Nation.

Shorten's approval rating lifts two points, to 39. It is his best number since March 2015. Morrison loses one point in the preferred prime minister rating, to 45. Shorten is up two points, to 37.

Morrison sees pictures of Shorten visiting a child-care centre in Stirling, a marginal electorate in Perth. Five children are gathered in a circle in front of the Labor leader. Another sits on Plibersek's lap. "I hear he is reading a book to children today," Morrison says. "It wasn't *The Cranky Bear*, disappointingly. It was *The Hungry Caterpillar*. He will be hungry, chomping into your wallet, chomping into your wallet to pay for his spend-a-thon."

Dan Tehan says the government will release its policies in the last three weeks of the campaign. He promises a low-taxing government. He says Labor will promise the world and strangle the economy. He says their policy for child-care workers is extraordinary.

He says, "It's basically an arrangement where they are bribing unions to go and stand at child-care centres and tell people to vote for Labor."

He says, "I've never seen the like of it. They cannot explain the policy. We don't know where it will lead to. What other sectors are they going to use taxpayers' money to pay for wage increases? This is extraordinary. And it is just purely and utterly a bribe to the unions."

He says, "This is a fast track to a socialist, if not communist, economy."

*

Miranda Devine writes that the debate starts nervously for Shorten. He scribbles notes. A page drops to the floor between him and Morrison.

"Bill Shorten surprised everyone," she writes, "even himself, last night when he won the first head to head televised debate against Prime Minister Scott Morrison."

She writes that Shorten droned on about child care, dental health and climate change. Morrison took charge by asking him to cost his policies. She writes that Shorten was annoyed: that he was peevish and sniping. He didn't know the cost of a Nissan Leaf electric car.

She writes that Morrison's best moments came on border security. She says he was on a roll when it came to wages and landed a blow on franking credits.

"But half an hour in, something changed in Shorten," she writes. "He put down the clipboard and loosened up. No more Mr Nice Guy."

He asks why Morrison voted eight times against higher penalty rates. He gets in a joke about Clive Palmer's preferences. He calls him a Good Samaritan, the unicorn of Liberal politics. The audience laughs. He hits his stride.

"He had won the room," Devine writes. "Afterwards, Shorten walked straight past his wife Chloe to shake hands with every member of the audience. The Prime Minister followed suit briefly before leaving early. Shorten stayed on to bask in his relief."

*

Steve Dickson resigns from One Nation's Queensland Senate ticket. He was filmed in a strip club in Washington with a man he thought was a National Rifle Association of America lobbyist.

"The footage shown does not reflect the person I am. It shows a person who was drunk and not in control of his actions and I take full responsibility for allowing that to happen," he says. "I informed my wife, Debbie, the following morning that I had attended a strip club in Washington, DC, and that I had too many drinks and little recollection of the night. She accepted that and after viewing the footage, I am thankful that she is standing by me."

Dickson grabs at a woman's breast. He stands over another and slides a note into her underwear.

"I think white women fuck a whole lot better," he says. "They know what they're doing. Asian chicks don't. I've done more Asian than I know what to do with."

He tells a dancer to touch his penis. She declines.

"She's keen," he says. "I think. Mate, I don't know. You fucking ask her."

*

People are taking photographs with Shorten's red bus. The text promises "A fair go for Australia." Shorten's lips are thinner than they are in real life. The decal is pasted over the Murrays Coaches logo and the old "s" is just visible, twisting between his teeth.

A staffer says the negative press hurts. "Sometimes, it feels like you're getting body-slammed."

*

Seven key independents issue a statement of environmental demands. Their support in a hung parliament would be contingent on these points. They call the document a "climate leadership agreement."

The agreement opposes the opening up of the Galilee Basin and specifically Adani's Carmichael Mine. It calls for restored funding to the Climate Change Authority, to enable it to act as an independent scientific advisory body. It calls for Australia to exceed its Paris commitments, to not use carryover credits, to be drawing half its power from renewables by 2030, and to have a road map for an entirely renewable power market. It calls for increased investment in clean energy and refuses to support government subsidies for fossil fuels.

"We recognise this is not an exhaustive list of actions we could take, but it represents a starting point towards making the Australian Parliament a greater force for responsible and effective climate action."

The agreement is signed by Andrew Wilkie in Clark, Kerryn Phelps in Wentworth, Julia Banks in Flinders, Helen Haines in Indi, Zali Steggall in Warringah, Rob Oakeshott in Cowper and Oliver Yates in Kooyong.

*

The Liberal candidate for Isaacs says there are ways of dealing with Islam that are commonly overlooked. "Stop supporting Islam with government money," he says, "and enforce the citizenship laws."

Writing on *Quadrant*, he says Australia should not accept an oath of allegiance sworn by a Muslim. "A Muslim is a person who subscribes to an ideology which requires the following," he writes: "killing or enslavement of the citizens of Australia if they do not become Muslim, replacing the Australian government and legal systems with Sharia, lying about their purposes to conceal their activities." He says this ideology depends on the "payment of protection money by non-Muslims to Muslims" in the form of unemployment benefits, disability support, child endowments and sickness benefits. He says, "They are clearly people of bad character."

He says governments should stop funding Islamic schools. "The various Australian governments must stop giving money to organisations which are essentially fomenting rebellion against the government."

When the comments are reported, he is disendorsed. "Those comments were entirely wrong," he says, "and I apologise unreservedly for them."

A few hours later, the Liberal candidate for Wills resigns. He has made a submission to the government's religious freedom review, warning against homosexuality. "The dangers and health risks have been well documented in many reliable medical sources for years."

Earlier, he said he wished he had been at the preselection of Tim Wilson, so he could have prevented his appointment. His logic was simple: "No homosexual MP."

He said the Liberal Party needed the "Godly god."

A coffee comes for Shorten. "Back to the story," he says.

The question is about Christchurch. Twelve days earlier, an Australian man walked into two mosques in New Zealand and killed fifty worshippers. He live-streamed the murders on social media. Has the massacre changed the election? Has it challenged the anxieties on which conservatives can campaign?

"I don't know that yet," Shorten says. "I think it all goes to the bigger issue: what's your view about Australians? Do you appeal to the better angels of our nature, or their fears? It's all a sub-play to that story. What do you think about the Australian people? Do you think they're big-minded and tolerant, or fearful and insecure? We're all a blend of all of that. It's all about that."

Christchurch fundamentally altered this campaign. The fear on which every election since Tampa had been fought was suddenly a poison. The playbook was torn up. Candidates were being disendorsed for views that once had a seat in cabinet. Anti-Islamic rhetoric could no longer be seen as different to anti-Islamic violence. The Morrison campaign was stalled by it.

"Well, you can say that," Shorten responds. "I don't think I can politically analyse – well, I should politically analyse – the consequences of Christchurch … For me, it's just a tragedy."

*

The roll is unusually full. The electoral commission says it is the most complete in the country's history. Youth enrolments rose hugely under Tony Abbott. They rose again, to a lesser degree, before the postal vote on same-sex marriage. Still, a third of the roll is aged over sixty.

In the first three days of pre-polling, 375,000 people cast their votes. At the last election, at this point, the number was 225,000. By polling day, the figure is 4.76 million. With postal votes, it's almost 40 per cent of the roll. People just want it to be over.

*

On a billboard in Rockhampton, Shorten says he doesn't support the Adani project. Next to the quote is a photo of Shorten holding a "Stop Adani" banner.

The picture has been retouched to disguise the fact he is pulling the banner out of the hands of a protester. The quote is out of context, too: he says he doesn't support the mine, but he wouldn't stop it.

Labor says Adani is killing them in Queensland. They can feel the numbers going backwards. The billboard is in Herbert. The seat is held on a margin of thirty-seven votes.

*

In Lyons, in Tasmania, the Liberal candidate resigns. Yesterday, Scott Morrison said he believed her anti-Islam posts were doctored. More emerged overnight.

She admits to some posts and not others. In one, she responds to a speech Shorten gave at a republic rally. Malcolm Roberts had shared an image of Shorten talking with the Indigenous flag behind him, asking where the flag of Australia was. "I couldn't give a shit about whether or not we have a queen," she wrote. "I care about our safety. How about we have a referendum on whether or not we close our borders to Muslims?"

By midafternoon, the Labor candidate for Melbourne has also resigned. A rape joke he had shared online is printed in the media, as well as a joke about the vaginas of lesbians. He had been sitting at the front of Shorten's women's speech. He was in the photographs afterwards. "I think this is a really important lesson for young people," he says, "that your social media footprint will follow you."

*

When Morrison speaks in numbers, that's all there is. Context leaves him. Figures overwhelm the words. "For those earning over forty thousand for the big change, which is having the same tax rate going down from thirty-two and a half cents down to thirty cents for between forty thousand and two hundred thousand, the bill for that is ninety-six," he says during the second debate. "The bill for actually extending the tax threshold from thirty-seven to forty-five – the bill for that is forty-six thousand."

Morrison won't give a figure for the money going to the top income bracket. Shorten writes one on a piece of paper and holds it up for the cameras: $77 billion. "I'm happy to decode the question," Shorten says. "What is the top income bracket 2024–25 and how much is that going to cost for the remainder of the medium term? Seventy-seven billion dollars to the top 3 per cent of earners. It's nice money if you can get it."

Shorten wins the second debate, albeit narrowly. He smiles through the answers. He is easy on his feet, putting his finger to his chin as the prime minister speaks. He sees the bully rise in Morrison and doesn't rise to it. He shows the quality rarest in him: comfort.

EVERYMEN DON'T EXIST

Mitch Fifield is waiting at the police youth club in Bateau Bay. He has his hands on his hips and is standing alone. There is a mural off to one side, of an eagle and a boy surfing. The announcement is of new penalties for internet trolling. There will be new regulations for digital products and a digital platforms inquiry should the government be re-elected. There is little of significance and no new money.

A Healthy Harold igloo has been inflated on the basketball court and a brace of children arranged for the cameras. Healthy Harold lessons are not ordinarily taught here, but the venue has been organised at the last minute. The children have been pulled together from local sports clubs. The giraffe mascot itself is in Parramatta: the weekend's league game still takes precedence. Morrison is not answering questions from the media today, but he is making images.

"Hello, kids," he says as he arrives. "What have you got there?" He steps towards the smallest boy in the crowd, who has something under his shirt. The cameras drop with Morrison. "It's Thomas the Tank. Can I have a look?" The boy produces a blue locomotive. It looks as if it has been sucked on. The boy looks at it, then offers it to the prime minister. "Well," Morrison says, "you have played with that a lot."

Morrison's wife, Jenny, helps him speak to the children. He makes an effort to always be moving. His face is oddly smooth and when he speaks his bottom lip does the greatest share of work. He crawls inside the igloo to sit in on a class. It is about cyber safety. Most of the media waits outside. You can hear the teacher quieting the children. Morrison speaks the loudest. "This is a different kind of bubble," he says from within the igloo. "The kind of bubble I like."

Officers from the federal police guard the igloo full of children and the prime minister. There is only one entrance, so they stand either side of it. Ben Morton is here, the member for Tangney, in Western Australia. They call him the prime minister's watcher. He travels everywhere with

Morrison. He has on a chequered button-down and hemmed blue jeans and looks fifteen years older than he is. "I'm really focused on what our task is at hand," he says. "But good luck with the essay. They're important pieces."

An adviser goes into the igloo: "I'm just going to ask him to come out." Morrison emerges, smiling. "That's the sort of bubble I don't mind," he says again for the cameras. "I think that's a helpful bubble."

The children follow him out. Their parents are waiting. Morrison rolls his shoulders when he stands. The tail of his tie reaches not quite to his sternum. He has taken off his jacket: his paunch is oversatisfied and his nipples are erect. "Who's got any questions for me or for Mitch?" he asks. "Not the media. You'll get your chance later."

There are no questions. Jenny goes to the bathroom. Morrison shakes hands with everyone. "Thanks very much. Thanks for coming along."

As he works the background, a television reporter starts her cross: "The Coalition wants heftier penalties for anyone who trolls people online ..."

*

At the Labor launch in Brisbane, Penny Wong receives an enormous cheer. Shorten calls her a weapon. She is sharp and crisp. Everything she says lands. She envisages an Australia that is generous and serious.

"The Liberals and the Nationals and their far-right alliance don't care about the diversity and the unity we've all worked so hard for here in Australia," she says. "They don't cherish the progress we've made, progress I've seen in my own lifetime. And they will compromise it all, and they will give it all away, for nothing more than a handful of votes in a handful of seats from a handful of haters. And this isn't just something the conservative parties do; it has become who they are."

Chloe Shorten introduces her husband as caring, smart, funny and gentle. She says he is a great listener. Her voice is small and worn and convincing. "He's driven by a determination to make a difference for those who need it," she says. "My friends, I know how much this party means to Bill. I know how much your support means to him. And I know he leads a group of extraordinary people who with your help will be a great, great government for this country of ours."

Before he speaks, he kisses Chloe on both cheeks and shakes hands with Tanya Plibersek. He promises a better deal for the next generation. He mentions dental care and early childhood learning. He says there will be real action on climate change. He says theirs will be a government focused on serving the people of Australia. "This is the choice for every citizen of our great nation: three more years of smug, smirking, unfair complacency under the conservatives, or a bolder, better and more equal future for Australia under a new Labor government."

It works in the room.

*

When you stand very close to Scott Morrison, he is just as ordinary as he appears on television. Before he arrives, Jenny tells the audience he is a loyal and trustworthy person. They met at the age of twelve and married at twenty-one. "My first impression of Scott was that he was really confident and a very cute boy. It was, like, in Year 7 and Year 8. That's really all that mattered, how cute someone was. I think there's a lot more to him now."

This is the largest meeting the Terrigal branch of the Liberal Party has ever held. The room has low ceilings and helium balloons and pitchers of iced water on the bar at the back. There are gold watches and men with sweaters over their shoulders. A man in wraparound sunglasses has had a suit made the same colour as the campaign t-shirts. He stands to have his picture taken.

The local member, Lucy Wicks, says Morrison's father was a police officer and his brother is an ambulance driver. She says Jenny is trained as a nurse.

"Service is sort of ingrained in Scott, his family," Jenny says. "I'd say in my family. Service to the community. His father was in local council. He was the mayor of Waverley for a while. That's where Scott got, I think, his love and taste for politics."

Jenny says he is a soft touch with their children. She says the girls have him wrapped around their fingers. "I want people to know that Scott is an – he will fight for you," she says. "What things are on your mind. He will listen to you. He will take everything on board. And he will go in to bat for you. He is tenacious. He's stubborn. And he's doggedly determined. So if he believes in something, he is going to go straight down and fight for you. For what you need and what you want for a better life for your families. He's a good, honest, compassionate person. That's the Scott I know."

*

Morrison enters to the song "Hotshot" by Gyom, who writes music for phone apps and branding campaigns. The prime minister is described as a friend of the Central Coast. There is a long applause. "It's great to be here on the Central Coast," he says. "I love being on the Central Coast. Love it."

There is a high table with a single bottle of water on it. Morrison walks back and forth across the stage. He has a performer's energy. The cliché of the televangelist is hard to avoid. "How good is Lucy Wicks?" he shouts over the cheering. "How good is Lucy Wicks? And just quietly, how good is Jenny Morrison?"

He puts his hand in his pocket and calls his wife a blessing. He modulates his voice. He knows how to speak quietly. He calls on seriousness. It has the feeling of an act but it has the showmanship of a good one. He says visiting here reminds him of the simple things that make Australia great. He describes a vision of Australia, of humble people with decent aspirations.

"We have aspirations to get a job, be well trained and educated, start a family, support your kids, pay your taxes, live in your community and make your community stronger, making a contribution, not taking one, not seeking to anyway, and understanding that there are those less fortunate than ourselves, who we support, because that's what we do in Australia."

He points his finger to make a point. "We have the aspiration to buy a home and to make a home. Not just buy one, but to make one: for our kids, for our families, for our friends. This is where we live. We come together in our homes. Our homes are very important to us. Menzies talked about homes as not just materials. Homes that go well beyond just the four walls in which we live and the landscaping out the front, which is nice to have."

He fills out his hand, as if he is holding something to his chest. "The value in your home is important. It's the biggest investment, biggest thing you will buy in your life for most Australians. Certainly that's the case for Jenny and I. It means a lot and people shouldn't play around with that and undermine it."

He says the final aspiration of all Australians is to save for their retirement. He looks for faces in the room. He makes eye contact. "This is a fundamental, decent, honest aspiration. You know, in the Liberal Party, we get aspiration. We understand it. Because we live it. It's our stories."

His hand is turned outwards now in rapture. "It's the stories that we live. It's the stories our families live. It's the stories our parents live. It's the stories we want our children to live as we raise them up. That they understand that having an aspiration – and having these decent, honest, simple goals – is nothing to sneer at. It's something to celebrate. I tell you what, it's also not something you should tax."

He waits on the applause. There are teacups placed at the side of the room, like in an Olive Cotton photograph. "Bill Shorten and Labor want to tax the honest, decent aspirations of Australia because they don't know how to manage money. I have a plan and my government has a plan and my team has a plan to celebrate and back in the aspirations of hard-working Australians."

He gets a cheer for his tax cuts. He says money is better off in the hands of people, not governments. He says these cuts are not a cost to the budget. The smell of ammonia comes from the beer taps at the back. "It's not a cost," he says. "It's your money. And you should keep it."

He says the last time Labor delivered a surplus was the year Taylor Swift was born. He says it takes a long time to shake off their mismanagement. He tries the line twice. A woman turns to the old man next to her: "It's a song."

The biggest cheer he gets is for announcing his government has cancelled the visas of 4400 people and sent them home. He says many of them were paedophiles. He says when Labor was in power, this wasn't happening. "At this election," he says, "we have to stop the Labor Party from taking your choices away by taking your hard-earned money away."

Morrison works here. His face is on the corflutes alongside the local member's. In this room there is no doubt: he has won the election.

*

Pictures come through of the Labor launch. The press bus is excited to see Kevin Rudd seated next to Julia Gillard. They see the grab of Paul Keating calling Morrison "a fossil with a baseball cap." They play it over and over. He has won the day. "Keating's the sort of guy who would walk in naked to a swingers' party," a journalist says. "He doesn't care. He ratchets it straight up."

Shorten has two signatures, one for bank cheques and another for the public. For the first he is "W.R." and for the second he is "Bill." The letters are placed close together and in each he is careful not to take up too much room. The only flamboyance is the "S" in his surname, which loops over on itself and reaches up to catch the top of the "h" that follows.

Shorten wishes his writing was better. "I'd always have liked to have better handwriting," he says. "I always envied those really joined-up running writing people." He got his second signature when he was an articled clerk. He wanted people to know who had written to them. "Does it surprise you?" He sounds worried, perhaps uncertain: "What's the import of that question?"

Morrison's signature has shifted four times since he became prime minister. In its latest form, it is a cursive "ScoMo." Shorten is suddenly doubting of his answer. "That doesn't, that doesn't mean, though, that I'm not capable of learning," he says. "See, one of the reasons I thought the Turnbull premiership might be a failure, I thought, what can you teach a rich white guy who is a multimillionaire in their sixties? What's going to change? How is he going to be radically different? And if the composite of his personality led his colleagues to get rid of him once, unless he's had a radical makeover, it's the same problems. I think you learn a lot more. I reconsider my views and I look at things and I update my logic."

*

Morrison tells Alan Jones that action on climate change is not the issue. The issue is Bill Shorten, who won't tell the country what his policy will cost. He says Shorten doesn't know the price of anything because he doesn't have to pay it. It's the opposite of Oscar Wilde's definition of a cynic.

Jones agrees with him. He plays a tape of a caller saying Shorten is an idiot. The caller says the Labor leader is a goose, and that he doesn't understand the real facts of the economy: that it is based on the building game, and that climate action will destroy it.

Jones says the impact on the economy is unsustainable. He says "surely," to make it a question. He laughs at the idea of electric cars.

"The thing is that Bill thinks he can make everything free without anyone having to pay for it," Morrison says. "We saw that again on the weekend. We've seen it day in and day out on this campaign. He's spending like there's no tomorrow and apparently it's not going to cost anything. Well, it is. Your listeners. The retirees are going to be taxed twenty-seven times harder than multinationals under Bill Shorten's policies."

Morrison's bus calls it "the infomercial." Jones's talent is in convincing his audience that the prime minister needs him more than he needs the prime minister. Morrison makes it look easy. Jones leads him through the interview as Simpson guided his donkey.

On talkback, Morrison sounds like a man among his people. Radio is his medium. His voice is sure and convincing. He listens well for the cues of his host. "Great line," Jones tells him when he starts quoting a Little Doer Carpets commercial. "Great line."

This is where Morrison is narrowing the polls. This whole election, he has made a virtue of the unremarkable. He has nothing to sell and the emptiness can be mistaken for honesty.

"Julia Gillard and Kevin Rudd – they were all there at the launch on the weekend," Morrison says. "What that reminded me of was just all of those failed programs they had when they were in government. Because Labor is spending an enormous amount of money. Huge amounts of money they're planning to spend ... They think they can solve everybody's problems by spending your money."

*

Arthur Sinodinos says the election is a crapshoot. He's in a car park in Nowra, waiting for Morrison. "The momentum has been with us at different times, especially in Queensland," he says. "Central Queensland, even the outer suburbs of Brisbane. It's a narrow pathway to victory, with the odds going the other way. But it ain't over until it's over."

Despite everything, Arthur Sinodinos has an honest face. He does not look confident.

Sinodinos was chief-of-staff to John Howard. His bearing is that of a man in a back office. He says, "Victoria's where the problem is."

Morrison arrives through a knot of maritime unionists. They are protesting his announcement of funding for an "Australian Made" campaign. "Jobs not logos," they shout into a loudspeaker. "Scott Morrison has the hide to come back to our region and tell us he's going to fix it with an Australian Made logo. It's not the logo that's the problem, prime minister. It's the flags on our vessels."

A Liberal branch member shouts back, an older man with long, straight legs. "Go back to Port Kembla, you fat cat," he says to one of them. "You want to pay everyone so that no one has jobs."

Morrison wears a lot more make-up than Shorten. He moves a full ninety degrees while he is talking, to make sure everyone has the shot. The chemical factory he is visiting specialises in water treatments and products for babies. He puts on an orange vest and walks into the first shed. As he makes small talk with the workers, unpacked bottles of headlice lotion follow on down the conveyor belt.

In the next shed, he points at things and asks questions. There is a big silver tank and he confirms that it is expensive. A rosella is trapped inside and flies into the wall again and again. Morrison finds a trolley with an unplugged emulsifying pump on it and wheels it a little way out onto the factory floor. He puts his foot up on the trolley and waits for the cameras to get what they need.

He stands in front of a pallet of orange foaming handwash. The sleeve of his jacket is worn: the lining has fused with the fabric. He says the country is working out Bill Shorten. He says the country can't risk big programs. He says spending is a risk and so is tax. "Now is not the time, certainly not the time, to be engaging in these big policy experiments."

At Shellharbour Hospital, he reannounces $128 million for redevelopment. The project is already in the budget. The front of the hospital has already been dug up. The building smells of bacon and melting cheese. The renal facility where he holds his press conference is mouldering. "I'm just going to look at the plans," he says, indicating a blueprint on one wall. "Good luck with it. We're glad to be able to provide the support."

Sinodinos follows a few paces behind as Morrison walks through the day ward. He is smiling. "I feel sorry for the patients," he says.

*

In Albury, a young woman throws an egg at the prime minister. It doesn't break.

"My concern about today's incident in Albury was for the older lady who was knocked off her feet," Morrison says. "I helped her up and gave her a hug. Our farmers have to put up with these same idiots who are invading their farms and their homes."

The Intergovernmental Science-Policy Platform on Biodiversity and Ecosystem Services releases a report saying a million species are at threat of extinction. The report is unparalleled in its scale. It blames land clearing but also climate change and pollution. "Biodiversity – the diversity within species, between species and of ecosystems – is declining faster than at any time in human history," it says.

The same day, Morrison warns about what he calls "green tape." He says Labor will use it to take people's jobs. "They want to hypercharge an Environment Protection Authority, which will basically interfere and seek to slow down and prevent projects all around the country," he says. "We believe there should be responsible, practical, environmental regulations that protect and safeguard our environment, and of course they should be in place, but we're very cautious when it comes to unaccountable bureaucracies that can, at the end of the day, destroy the opportunities for businesses to create jobs."

The Coalition doesn't have a genuine climate policy. Morrison says he believes in climate change but he also believes in the economy. He says we will meet Paris targets. Labor's strategy is the Coalition's old strategy, slightly improved. It is a hedge.

There is support for a referendum on an Indigenous Voice to Parliament, but it is not advanced during the campaign. A story in *The Australian* likens it to Brexit. There is limited talk about industrial relations and only late in the campaign is there discussion of the arts or the public broadcaster. The Coalition plans cuts to both.

Although Labor's platform is broad, the election ends up being about very little: lower taxes under the Coalition or spending on health and early childhood.

In Albury, the woman is charged with common assault and possession of cannabis.

*

At a meeting with the NSW Business Chamber in Parramatta, Morrison warns that Shorten would surrender businesses to the Australian Council of Trade Unions. In particular, he warns about the council's secretary. "Sally McManus will now be a board member, figuratively, on every single one of your companies," he says. "The union movement will basically be in control of your businesses if the Labor Party is elected. They will be the ones who give final approval of what can you do with your businesses. So much for you running your business if Bill Shorten is elected. They want control of the Australian building industry again. They want control of every site. They want control of every decision you make.

"If Bill Shorten is prime minister, you can be sure Sally McManus will get her way."

*

Bob Hawke and Paul Keating make a joint statement, their first in twenty-eight years. A few weeks earlier they had met for tea served in wide china cups and biscuits set out on dessert plates. Craig Emerson was there and took a picture.

"It is a blatant denial of history for Scott Morrison to allege that the Labor Party cannot manage the economy," they say in the statement, "when he knows the design and structure of the modern Australian economy was put in place exclusively by the Labor Party." And, later on: "Let's examine what the Prime Minister declares he has on offer as an economic strategy for the next three years and beyond. As far as we can see, two things and two things only: a trickle-down economic policy where if the wealthy accumulate more wealth, some of it may trickle down to the workforce; and unfunded tax cuts five years away. Yet on these paltry foundations, with the economy dribbling along at about half its growth potential, with real wages frozen and with no growth strategy, the Prime Minister repeats his bald-faced claim that the Labor Party can't manage the economy."

They end with an endorsement of Shorten's platform: "Labor governments are best seen as a continuum of reform, each building on the achievements of its predecessors. When we look at the quality of the personnel and the policy agenda of the current leadership of our party, we do so with pride and confidence that if they get the opportunity, they will be a government that can provide the type of leadership that Australia so desperately needs and that the Liberal Party is singularly incapable of providing."

At the same time, Keating is saying in private that he cannot see how Labor will win. He can't get the numbers to add up.

*

The response Shorten gives is ten minutes long. Twice he is tearful. "I'm going to take a little bit of time on this answer," he says. "And I thank you for asking it."

The question is about his mother. *The Daily Telegraph* has run a front-page piece doubting his account of her life. The headline is "Mother of Invention." The article says Shorten idolises his mother and repeatedly evokes her. It accuses him of trying to paint himself as downtrodden and working-class, avoiding her successes to do so. "Make no mistake – Shorten did not lie," it says. "But a glaring omission in his story means that he comes off as the slippery salesman yet again, playing straight into the Liberals' attack line."

Shorten's forehead is creased like roofing iron as he begins to speak. He talks about the catastrophic heart attack his mother suffered in her sleep. She never woke up. It was five years ago last month. "I miss her every day," he says.

He describes her upbringing in Melbourne, the eldest of four children, the daughter of a printer and a bookbinder. He says she wanted to study law, but that her family couldn't afford tuition. She took a teaching scholarship instead. He remembers how his Uncle George told him they would go to Station Pier in Port Melbourne and hold the streamers as the liners left port. His mum wanted to see the world.

He catches on the memory and starts to cry. The knowledge of her sacrifice is painful in his voice. "She taught in London," he says. "She was exposed to the Jesuits in London. That's why she sent me to a Jesuit school."

He says she did a PhD while she raised her sons and finally went to law school. She graduated at the top of her class. No one would take her for articles. She read for the bar, but in six years got only nine briefs. His eyes are wet at the thought of her embarrassment. "She discovered, in her mid-fifties, that sometimes you're just too old."

He calls her brilliant and says she is what drives him. People watching say it is an election-winning moment. "They play gotcha shit about your life story," he says, crying. "And more importantly, my mum's. I've spoken about my mum at length. I choose to give you that last bit of the battle of her time at the bar because my mum would want to say to older women in Australia: just because you've got grey hair, just because you didn't go to a special private school, just because you don't go to the right clubs, just because you're not part of some back-slapping boys' club, doesn't mean you should give up … My mum is the smartest woman I've ever known."

These are two wrongs he mentions, over and over: class and gender.

They are the slights that bound his mother's life and he has a child's certainty about changing them.

The *Telegraph* story was shopped by a staffer. It was rejected by at least two news outlets. When Morrison saw it, he said: "This is bad for us."

*

In Canberra, Chris Bowen releases Labor's costings. A lot of Labor's policies are his. He is furtive and diligent. He thinks. The negative gearing changes were led by him: he had to guide Shorten. "He brings hard ideas," a senior figure says. "He's the one bringing the economic strategy."

People in the party liken the relationship with Shorten to Keating as treasurer under Hawke. "You've got to remember: Hawke was Keating's biggest supporter until he wasn't."

Bowen says this is the earliest ever release of costings by an Opposition party. He is smiling and clean-shaven and the blinds behind him are drawn closed. His face is a continuous line, as if the cartoonist hasn't lifted his pen. The costings were produced by the Parliamentary Budget Office and checked by three independent accountants.

When he pauses, Bowen puckers his chin and his skin goes like a mandarin's. His costings show a surplus next financial year and every year over the forward estimates. They show a surplus of $21.7 billion by 2022–23, more than twice what the Coalition is promising.

"Australia has a two-class tax system," Bowen says. "If your income comes from a certain place, you have good accounting advice, you get access to the first-class tax system. If you are a normal payer, it is the very basic deductions, economy class, for you. We are reforming the tax system. These reforms raise $154 billion over the next decade."

On the front page of *The Australian*, Paul Kelly announces Labor is ready to govern. He says these costings close the loop: "a better budget surplus, huge social spending properly financed and a tax redistribution with a limit on the overall increase in taxation . . . they win on the spending and they win on the surplus."

The Melbourne Convention Centre is oddly empty. An older man changes into a Liberal t-shirt in the middle of the deserted concourse. Tim Wilson is standing to one side, dressed in chinos. He hands a white package to a campaign worker. Greg Hunt walks by with his empty shoulders and his cocker spaniel hair. Marise Payne kisses Simon Birmingham on the cheek and then does the same to Michaelia Cash. Melissa Price stands alone with her phone in one hand and her arms behind her back. The most senior Liberal in the room is Nick Greiner, the party president and former NSW premier. The cameras do not notice him as he comes in.

The plenary is only one-third full. The stage is empty except for a perspex lectern and a man-sized flag, standing limp and near the back. Jenny Morrison walks on in a magenta dress, leading her two daughters. Her mother-in-law is there in a white blazer. "My name is Marion Morrison, and I'm Scott's mum," she says. "You already know Jenny and Abbey and Lily. And now I would like to welcome my son." Jenny leans forward to the microphone: "My husband." And the children: "Our dad."

Morrison climbs the stairs to the stage with two bouquets of flowers. He gives one to his wife and other to his mother. "Aren't they fantastic?" he says. "How good's Mum?"

He thanks his colleagues, thanks his friends. "They're the women in my life," he says as his mother and his wife leave the stage. "I couldn't love them more if I tried. And they couldn't love me more if they tried. Happy Mother's Day, Mum. Happy Mother's Day, Jen."

Morrison talks about the surety of selfless love. His voice has the flatness of the self-evident. He talks about his parents. He says how they lived in a house with his great-aunt, how they weren't rich. He says how he shared a room with his brother. He says that for forty-five years his mother volunteered at Girls' Brigade every Thursday and Friday night and his father volunteered at Boys' Brigade for just as long. He says they saved and planned and sacrificed. He says his mother is a woman of quiet and practical faith.

The experience is so religious that when he says his father is up there listening, you have to remember he means in Sydney.

Morrison doesn't have the energy of his usual performance. His hands are modest. He talks about Australia as if it is a country of first names. He mentions Christopher and Gav working in Gladstone, both in a family business. He mentions a couple in Wauchope with a new house. He mentions Maryanne, a woman in Melbourne who started her own weddings business. He talks about Roselea, who he hasn't met, a retired schoolteacher in Perth who lives on franking credits. He talks about Donna in northern Tasmania, whose son, Luke, has cystic fibrosis. A drug that was listed on the PBS last Father's Day means he can run without becoming breathless. There is a cheer for this. Morrison mentions Jacqueline and Robert, who lost their cows to flood and pneumonia. All he could do was hug her and promise he would not leave without her knowing they would rebuild. The country he describes is like a congregation. Danger is everywhere. There are curses to be broken. People are raised up and healed.

"Australia really is the best country in the world to live," he says. "I believe it is more than that. I believe that Australia is a promise to everyone who has the great privilege to call themselves an Australian. You know what that promise is. We know what it is. It is the promise that allows Australians, quietly going about their lives, to realise their simple, honest and decent aspirations. Quiet, hard-working Australians. An Australia where if you have a go, you get a go. Where you're rewarded and respected for your efforts and contribution."

If there are any veterans here, he thanks them for their service. He says Australia is a hard-won promise made by the generations that went before. He says an economy is what people live in and he will keep it strong.

"I'm not getting into a spend-a-thon with Labor," he says. "They're welcome to it. Reckless spending is not a vision for Australia. It's a burden on current and future generations."

Morrison makes a policy announcement for first home buyers. They will be allowed to borrow with a deposit of only 5 per cent. There is new money for early childhood health. He makes a promise on private health insurance: that there will be no changes under his government. "I will not punish Australians for taking responsibility for themselves and their families." He says he and Jenny are committed to fighting youth suicide. "It's a curse on our nation and it's a curse we must break together."

He calls out to Birmo in South Australia and Dan on schools funding. He calls out to Alan Tudge and David Coleman for "keeping migration under control, which we must do." He calls out to Melissa and Angus on climate change. "We are doing our bit, as we should as a global citizen," he says. "But I'm not going to do it and put our people and our kids' economic future at risk."

He says Greg Hunt saved the Great Barrier Reef. He says to his daughters that the speech is almost over. If it is intended as homely confidence, it doesn't land. He says he never gets tired of mentioning Operation Sovereign Borders. He calls it a signature achievement. "Australians know that the Liberals and Nationals can always be trusted to keep Australians safe and our borders secure."

He leaves the stage holding his wife's hand. His mother is guided out through a side door. There is a curious vacancy in the room. Privately, Tony Abbott is telling people he will lose in Warringah. Senior Liberals fear Gilmore and Reid are gone. Farrer could be lost and Cowper, too. It looks likely they will not win back Wentworth.

In the foyer, a volunteer holds two cupcakes in each hand. They are oily and small, with icing piped on top and a little rice-paper badge that says "Liberal." The official figure on seating comes back: 430 people were there to see Scott Morrison launch his first campaign as prime minister. The overwhelming feeling is not one of victory.

*

Labor accidentally releases its talking points for the day. On the Coalition launch, it says Morrison has no vision for Australia. "The mere fact that Tony Abbott, Malcolm Turnbull and John Howard, Julie Bishop can't sit in the same room together says everything you need to know about the chaos and division engulfing the modern Liberal Party." The briefing document reminds Labor candidates that nothing Morrison says will make up for the past six years. It tells them to point to failure on climate change, failure on the cost of living and failure on wages. They should say: "It's time for change. Vote for Labor and vote for change." News Corp has been elevated to a topic heading alongside "costings" and "Angus Taylor." Labor's message of the day, which begins the briefing, is: "This election is a choice between Labor's strong, stable and united team and the Liberals' coalition of chaos with no vision for Australia."

*

Bill Kelty says Kim Beazley lost in the last week in 1998. He says that's because Beazley never believed he would win. "They've not won and there's a chance they could lose," he says.

Kelty's hair is soft and white. There is an imp in his voice. He is in hospital. Nothing serious, he says. Someone's just come in with a cake.

"There's one test in politics," he says, "and it's if you're genuine." He says Shorten has that: "He's just got to believe in himself."

Shorten knows doubt. He learnt it in the unions, learnt that accepting his own limits was the way to consensus.

"What he is not," Kelty says, "he's not as confident as Bob. He's not as smart as Whitlam. He's not as good an actor as Keating. He's running a different political strategy – it's a strategy that's not ever been run in this way by the Labor Party. He's running a big, team-based approach."

Kelty says Shorten found himself at the party's policy launch in Box Hill. "That was the place where he got his story together. He got the story right."

*

The final week's Newspoll has the two-party preferred at 49–51. Shorten's net approval rating is at a four-year high. Morrison is seven points ahead as preferred prime minister, but Shorten has his best number since the conservatives changed leaders. If the election were held today, Labor would win seventy-seven seats. The Coalition would be on sixty-eight.

Excepting the *Northern Territory News*, every Murdoch paper in the country editorialises in favour of a Morrison government. The Morrisons give an exclusive interview to News Corp. Morrison says his wife is a "love machine." She says people don't realise how funny he is: "They might not get to his humour, his softer side ... So people don't get to see that. I think they might find him a bit harder, maybe, because they don't get to know him. If everyone got to meet Scott in a pub, they would totally be – he'd just win them over."

Two days out from the election, Bob Hawke dies. Shorten says that when he saw him a few weeks ago he was doing a crossword in the sun. Hawke had asked how the election was going. "We have lost a favourite son," Shorten says. "Bob Hawke loved Australia and Australia loved Bob Hawke. But his legacy will endure forever."

Morrison says Hawke was a great intellect, with enormous passion and courage. "But it was his ability to connect with everyday Australians, with a word, with that larrikin wit, with that connection and an understanding of everyday Australian life, that we will most remember Bob Hawke."

A man with a plate of beef skewers comes out of the door where Shorten is expected. The crowd stirs. A drunk volunteer explains to the man next to her what went wrong.

On the stage, Shorten holds the lectern to steady his hands. "I know that you're all hurting," he says. "And I am, too."

It is just on eleven o'clock. The Coalition has not won, but it is clear Labor cannot form government. "This has been a tough campaign, toxic at times. But now that the contest is over, all of us have a responsibility to respect the result." As Shorten resigns, his eyes glisten. Chloe looks as if she has been crying. She keeps her hands folded low over her stomach. "Along with my family, my precious family, the Labor Party and the trade union movement – it's my life."

A woman wipes mascara across her cheek. Shorten says there is nothing more he could have done. He says their vision was clear and their reforms upfront. He mentions climate change. He mentions Medicare and wages and the treatment of women. He says parts of the country remain deeply divided. He says the preference deals with Palmer and One Nation hurt them in Queensland and New South Wales.

"Friends," he says, "I am disappointed by tonight's results. But I am not disappointed for me. I will always be proud of the courage and the integrity and the vision that our team showed. I'm disappointed for people who depend on Labor, but I'm proud that we argued what was right, not what was easy."

There is a point at which the largeness of a moment either overwhelms the people in it or makes them large, too. Bill Shorten stays exactly the same size.

"It is what it is," a staffer says to a reporter. "You can quote that."

*

In the room, they are chanting, "ScoMo." His daughters are working out on which side of him they should stand. Morrison extends God's blessings to Shorten and Shorten's family. Jenny laughs at his jokes. She throws her head backwards. "How good is Australia?" he says. "And how good are Australians?"

Morrison smiles and his teeth look surprised. His youngest daughter holds her elbow. His eldest claps. The flag behind him is enormous. "These are the quiet Australians who have won a great victory tonight," he says. "Because it's always been about them … Tonight is not about me. It's not about, even, the Liberal Party. Tonight is about every single Australian who depends on their government to put them first."

He counts off his other miracles: Lindsay, Herbert, Bass, Braddon, Longman, Macquarie. He points his finger like a gun: "Pretty much the whole state of Queensland." His tie is powder-blue and the pin on his lapel makes him look like a travel agent. He doesn't mention a single policy. The struggle with Morrison is to know what he wants, other than to be prime minister.

He says this is "a new make, a new model, a new way for us to campaign." It "has set an entirely new benchmark." He says, "We've got a lot of work to do, and we are going to get back to work, we're going to get back to work for the Australians that we know go to work every day, who face those struggles and trials every day. They're looking for a fair go, they're having a go, and they're going to get a go from our government." He finishes: "We are an amazing country, with amazing people. God bless Australia."

He kisses his daughter's head and waves to the faithful.

*

Labor's polling tells them they lost with the over sixty-five vote. It was the franking credits scare, the spectre of a retirement tax. The fear of unannounced death duties hurt, too. People in the party say they are not equipped to understand the generational divide, much less bridge it. They believed in the rightness of their policy: they thought the fairness of it was convincing enough. Tragedy is what happens when half the world is comfortable.

Strategists say the election was never unlosable. This wasn't 1993. They say the country is stuck on the same dividing line, on a vote that has been basically static since 2013. The regions are separated completely from the cities. Something will give but they don't know what.

Kevin Rudd blames Rupert Murdoch. He calls him the elephant in the room. "Murdoch … ran the single most biased campaign in Australian political history." He says there is silence about this. "People are in fear of Murdoch's power."

Shorten's initial analysis is simple: "We didn't get enough votes."

The published polls were three points out on the Coalition's primary. They were especially wrong in Queensland and Victoria. The final two-party split was 50.9–49.1.

Senior operatives say Labor lost on advertising. They say they might have won if they had a popular leader. In among the upset, these are the two points of agreement: their advertising didn't counter the Coalition's, and Shorten was too unpopular to win. He continued to set the course and few told him to change it. "Two weeks out we knew we were fucked."

Bill Kelty says the position on climate change was right but they needed a clearer transition for jobs. It cost them Queensland. He says the policy on franking credits was too risky. It cost them retirees. He says the economic package was too much about spending and not enough about actual reform. The whole policy agenda was contingent on three savings measures. "Everything else he did was right. He won the debates, he put up a package, he was brave." Kelty says despite the scale of the agenda, there were no gains for Labor. "The result is sad but the primary vote – that's the tragedy."

The Coalition says Labor's agenda was too broad. They know their slogans cut through. They won because they were able to frame everything as a run on taxes. Matt Canavan calls it a workers' revolt: "This has been high-vis workers' revolution. They are the most visible Australians … but they are often ignored by our nation's political leaders."

Labor says this isn't the end of policy elections. They say policy is the only thing they can win on. They mention climate change and tax reform. "The outcome is one of the closest in Australian history. The disaster was that we thought we would win. This is not a big, warm embrace of Morrison. We lost the campaign because they succeeded in characterising our agenda as kicking the shit out of people on tax and we didn't counter it in our advertising. They made it seem like we would tax the buggery out of everyone." One Nation was a factor in Queensland and Palmer was a factor nationally. It wasn't his preferences: it was the scale and effectiveness of his advertising campaign against Labor. "I'm sick of the media saying Palmer won nothing. He won them the fucking government."

*

Shorten says the life he has chosen is a selfish one. He has asked for outsized sacrifices from his wife and children. He says he doesn't know how to justify it. "How does anyone?" he asks. "You could justify the ends. You could say the ends justify the means. You can compartmentalise and not think about it. You can say I'll make up for it later."

He says his hope is that he does not repeat the mistake. He won't say what the mistake is. "Try not to repeat the mistake. Learn. Learn, learn, learn," he says. "I sometimes think I should back my judgment more. Being talked off doing things. But I can't complain lately. I don't know, when … I'll have to think about that. But certainly what I've said stands, but I'll think about it a bit more, rather than give an answer off the top of my head."

Morrison gets up the morning after and goes to church. He spends his afternoon in the stands, watching the Cronulla Sharks. He drinks beer from a plastic cup and poses for photographs with other fans. At one point, he takes off his scarf and helicopters it above his head. He believes in a country that is comfortable. "I give thanks to live in the greatest country in all the world," he says. "Thanks again to all Australians all across the country."

Morrison's Australia is humble and the people in it are humble. That is the word he uses. Their aspirations are decent, honest, simple. They are nothing to sneer at. They are quiet, hard-working people. They are quietly getting on with life. The repetitions do not matter: the words all mean the same thing. These people are forgiven greed because what they want is not so much. Work entitles reward. Morrison fuses prosperity with virtue. He fuses himself to Howard and then to Menzies. The only glimpse of a future is in the retirement for which you are already saving.

"You know what that promise is," he says. "We know what it is. It is the promise that allows Australians, quietly going about their lives, to realise their simple, honest and decent aspirations. Quiet, hard-working Australians. An Australia where if you have a go, you get a go. Where you're rewarded and respected for your efforts and contribution."

Generally, ambition comes from one of two places: insecurity or privilege. This is what the literature says. "That's a big theory isn't it?" Shorten says. "I'd like to take that on notice. So the general question of where does ambition come from, I'm not qualified to answer. I'd like to think about that."

The great truth of Bill Shorten is that he doesn't know himself. He hasn't settled his character. In that way, he is like the country: ill at ease and incomplete. It is not just what he hides – the ruthlessness, the bastardry: it's that there are parts of him he has never found. Had he been prime minister, he would have governed from insecurity for an insecure nation. He would have built consensus because that is the only real way to answer uncertainty. As it is, Australia has found comfort once again in a hardman who says everything is simple and some of you will be okay.

SOURCES

This essay was written on the campaign trail with Bill Shorten and Scott Morrison. I am thankful to their staffs and to Bill Shorten for his candour in answering my questions. Scott Morrison refused to be interviewed for this piece. I am grateful to Jane Cadzow and Deborah Snow, whose profiles of him I have drawn on in the text. The quotes on pages 9 and 13 are theirs.

Susan Carland

I felt something strange reading Rebecca Huntley's Quarterly Essay.

It was such a peculiar sensation to feel while reading about modern Australian politics that initially it confused me. I went back to re-read passages multiple times, trying to translate my disorientation. Was it the arguments provided? The history? The data? No, no and no. The writing was lucid, the narrative engaging, the statistics helpful. So why did I feel unsettled?

At first, I classified this foreign feeling as *hope*. I could barely remember the last time I felt hopeful when considering Australian politics, but the details of where the majority of Australians sat on numerous topics were a pleasant surprise. Despite what political and media battles imply, Rebecca shows that the majority of Australians supported the original Gonski reforms, more funding for the NDIS and Medicare, and reined-in corporate donations to political parties. Rebecca even showed that the majority of Coalition voters (let alone everyone else) say climate change is caused by humans.

This was deeply encouraging, and for a moment I climbed into a boat of hope that, unexpectedly, also had the majority of my fellow Australians sitting inside it. Most of us wanted similar things for the nation! I was not in the minority! In a democracy, the will of the people prevails, so surely these things will be respected by our political leaders!

But quickly I realised it wasn't hope that I was experiencing. At least, it wasn't hope alone. Grafted onto my hope was intense frustration.

The very thing that gave me hope – that the majority of Australians wanted good and helpful things – was the same thing that made me despair. Because these wishes were not being reflected by our politicians. Some issues had been kicked under the couch and ignored by our leaders; others had been completely overruled and the very opposite cause aggressively championed instead. Why are schoolchildren going on massive protests for greater commitments to protecting the environment in a desperate attempt to get politicians' attention, when these politicians already know this is what most voters want (and these same children are sneeringly dismissed by some politicians while they're at it)?

It feels embarrassingly naive to be perturbed by this, like mine is a childish, simplistic view of democracy. But at its most fundamental level, democracy is meant to be about reflecting the will of the people. While politicians cannot check in with their constituents before they make each and every decision, and while policy change can be difficult and slow, the sheer number of topics Rebecca lists that have majority support but have been dismissed, ignored, overridden or put in the too-hard pile by our leaders is confronting. Self-preservation alone would suggest that politicians should listen keenly to the majority, so as to best reflect their will – and best keep their jobs. Yet on a litany of diverse issues, they aren't listening. How has the will of the people been so misrepresented? And, more importantly, why?

We can speculate on the reasons: politicians prioritising internal factions and party-room squabbles ahead of public sentiment is one (the same-sex marriage survey may be the most extreme example of this). Politicians wanting to keep large donors with vested interests onside may be another. Myopic self-protection by politicians who don't want to be responsible for change that will take longer than a three-year election cycle could be another.

That there is support across party lines over a long list of issues that are not being embraced by our leaders should bother us, but perhaps for more reasons than are first obvious.

The neglect of these concerns, and the self-serving dance between politicians and the media when discussing them, has led many of us to believe we, the majority, are actually the bleeding-heart minority. Consistently seeing politicians argue against tackling climate change, for example, creates a cognitive dissonance within us. If politicians are so reluctant to act on (or in some cases, even believe in) man-made climate change, we tell ourselves, then the only explanation is that this is what a large proportion of the electorate wants. Why else would our leaders act in such a nonsensical way, but to uphold democracy? And so, as Rebecca reports, in our minds we triple the number of Australians who reject climate change, assuming it's 23 per cent when in reality it's less than 8 per cent.

This is perhaps the most concerning detail to come out of Rebecca's essay. Politicians' behaviour is jarring with our understanding of democracy, so to reconcile that within ourselves, we assume the problem is with other voters – that they must be the ones who reject man-made climate change or don't want to increase funding to the ABC. We project onto our fellow Australians the beliefs of our politicians. What this misplaced blame does to community cohesion cannot be underestimated. We are living in a time of profound social silos and tribalism, and this is being further entrenched by our politicians' behaviour. They are creating divisions among voters – for instance, by pitting Adani mine jobs against climate change action. And so instead of turning on the politicians who don't represent us, we turn on each other.

Tolkien warns, "False hopes are more dangerous than fears." As I consider the hope I first felt while reading Rebecca's essay and the systematic account of what the majority of us actually want (as opposed to what politicians imply we want), I wonder if that hope is misplaced and thus dangerous. After the recent election result, that would be an understandable conclusion to draw. But as Rebecca shows, while our belief in institutions, religions and politicians is falling off a cliff of resentment, we still believe in democracy. That belief is something we can have genuine hope in. And if our politicians continue to ignore what so many of us want, perhaps it is they who should be fearful.

Susan Carland

AUSTRALIA FAIR

Correspondence

James Walter

Rebecca Huntley's *Australia Fair* has two striking virtues. It reminds us of how important the mobilisation of belief is in politics. And it is a tonic for those of us who might think the absence of any productive action on worrying social problems over the past decade represents not only political incompetence but also public indifference. Yet the Coalition's win in the 2019 federal election raises profound questions about how to reconcile Huntley's evidence of a persisting public commitment to social democracy and the apparent repudiation of such a program by the electorate.

Huntley sets out to clear the ground, exploring public opinion to show that it is not resistance to reform or withdrawal from democratic engagement that are at issue, but a perception that political institutions and elites are failing to heed the clear opinion of majorities on our signal challenges: climate change, housing, immigration and the treatment of asylum seekers. Underlying this is an argument that, if only the people at large were listened to, the Australian commitment to social democracy – government that intervenes when necessary to ensure services are delivered, fairness and relative equality are sustained and market failure is addressed – would be acted upon.

Hers is an optimistic essay, acknowledging in the closing pages persisting hurdles, but clearly framed both in relation to the strength of opinion on these key issues, and a conviction that the time for a progressive renaissance is at hand – and, she hoped, almost certain to be delivered at the 2019 federal election. She does not oversimplify, recognising that the task can only be undertaken by a Labor government, and noting that though majority opinion is moving in the right direction on climate change, for instance, the public is "only inching" towards realising the scale of the threat it represents. In fact, a Lowy poll published since the essay was released, during the 2019 campaign, registered for the first time that climate change had reached the top of the list of public concerns:

had a tipping point been reached? Apparently not, if the recent election outcome is taken into account.

I wanted to believe that Huntley was right, and still hope her essay is widely read. Yet reading it in the midst of the 2019 election campaign – as the polls tightened – prompted me to confront some questions that it begs, to do with how beliefs are mobilised in politics.

The first is this: if one accepts Huntley's analysis of the progressive zeitgeist, then why is it that the Coalition government was so deaf to public demand? Well, of course it came to power on the back of Tony Abbott's war on "the great big tax" supposedly represented by emissions trading. It's not easy to backtrack after that, even as public attitudes move on, so thereafter the Coalition vigorously defended the status quo. It was also undoubtedly influenced by coal industry donations, lobbying and the strategic placement of industry insiders in ministers' offices, as has been well documented. But more important than all of that was that it was hobbled by wars over belief within the party. Huntley's focus on public opinion – polls and focus groups – does not sufficiently attend to the beliefs of party insiders and the dynamics among party activists and supporters.

Three research studies are indicative of the problem. Huntley cites CSIRO research that supports her contention about the growing support for government action on climate change. That research also hints at the divergence of conservatives from the mainstream, since it notes that conservative voters are less likely to believe that climate change is caused by human behaviour and less likely to think government should do more to address the issue. An earlier study, in 2012, by Kelly Fielding and others at the University of Queensland, sharpens this differentiation. It shows that among politicians, political party affiliation and ideology have a powerful influence on climate change beliefs, since centre-left and progressive parties exhibit beliefs more consistent with scientific consensus about climate change than non-aligned or conservative leaders, and that motivated social cognition (that is, accepting only information that accords with existing views) is a powerful factor among conservatives. Finally, new research published by Anika Gauja (University of Sydney) and Max Grömping (Heidelberg University) in 2019 demonstrates that there are not only differences between party supporters and the rest of us, but also between party supporters themselves. The stronger party identification becomes, the lower the congruence between the views of supporters and the broader public. Parties now can be conceptualised as a series of concentric circles of increasing engagement but declining representativeness.

This clarifies the Coalition's predicament over recent years. In an age when the shared commitments that sustained mass parties have evaporated, leaders are relied on to stand in for the party, to speak for what it represents. Their success in doing so is evaluated by constant polling. But as party membership gets ever smaller, and residual true believers increasingly diverge from the mainstream, leaders are trapped. Abbott, arguably, faithfully represented the views of his party's most intense identifiers, and fatally lost public support. Turnbull instead spoke for what the public wanted – a more progressive program in general, including action on climate change – but each attempt to respond to popular demand provoked insurgency in the party room from those claiming (with some justification) to represent the beliefs of the party base. Has the task of satisfying both public expectations and party demands become impossible?

One might think that this is a problem only for the Coalition parties; that a change of government and the cold reality of Opposition might have forced the Liberals to adapt and to reform the party to recapture a broader, small "l" liberal constituency. That is to assume that the more progressive parties are immune from that dynamic of concentric circles, where party central turns out to be least in tune with the public at large. The research does not support that assumption.

Bill Shorten, as his equivocation during the campaign revealed, had his own difficulties in balancing the demands of some of those workers the ALP represents (in mining areas) with the public demand for climate action. Labor's lead in the polls tightened as, on one side, Queensland unionists worried about their jobs and, on the other, progressive climate activists rued his inability to go as far as some wanted. And while progressive parties now might be more attuned to the general directions of public opinion, the intense identifiers among them are prone to characteristic mistakes. Among the Greens, for instance, self-righteousness and the conviction that "most people" agree with them, at least on climate change, renders them blind to something Huntley also identifies: the pragmatic temperament of the Australian electorate.

Thus, at a time when the millennium drought had made the public receptive to a climate change message, the sainted Bob Brown refused to accept any pragmatic compromise and helped to spike Labor's first attempt at legislating emissions reductions in 2009 because it was not "good enough." It set the stage for a decade of climate wars. And there he was again this year, leading the Adani protest convoy, apparently oblivious that a tactic that plays well in St Kilda is completely counter-productive in Clermont, where, as one resident said, "Up here, coal is our economy. It is … everything!" Yes, Adani must be stopped, but to ride into town with an injunction, yet offer no suggestion for how to manage the transition to an alternative economic future, simply provoked derision: "Those guys have taken time off from their barista jobs and unemployment to drive up here in fuel-guzzling cars. I just think it's an insult, a slap in the face." It was a gift to the hard right struggling to hang on in those areas, encouraging some to bet that the egregious George Christensen would hold his marginal seat of Dawson. In the event, the election saw a swing of 11.26 per cent in favour of Christensen, with similar swings in adjoining coal-belt seats.

One other thing niggled away at my wish to share Huntley's optimism: reliance on what seem to be solid majority trends underestimates the way shifts at the margins can now be manipulated to destabilise "common sense." We have seen in Donald Trump's campaign and in Brexit how marginal and diverse minority opinion groups can be influenced through social media into aggregate coalitions of resentment and fear, leaching support away from commonly held views. The hired guns of opinion analysis have become experts at nudging belief to these ends. The Cambridge Analytica scandal was a stark instance. But our homegrown outfits working the same vein are no slouches. Crosby Textor's role in British elections and the Brexit "leave" campaign was notable, and Scott Morrison mentioned Lynton Crosby as among the "experts" he "listened to" while campaigning. More worryingly, it is clear that the big spending and disruptive tactics of Clive Palmer's UAP campaign, an overt instance of targeted messaging, were significant in influencing voting preferences to destroy Labor's chances in Queensland, as Laura Tingle persistently reminded us on election night. He won no seats, not even a seat in the Senate, but note what he gained: leverage over a government that will likely facilitate exploitation of coal reserves in the Galilee Basin in which not only Adani, but Gina Rinehart and Palmer himself hold mining tenements.

Despite mulling over these concerns, I, like most, persisted in believing that the consistency of Labor's apparent lead would ensure a win for progressives in 2019, but doubted there would be a landslide. It was not to be. And my concern about the disparity between public opinion and party insider belief underestimated the scale of the upset that eventuated. Labor's dreams were smashed. There will now be many debates about why. The immediate question for Huntley is whether the disjunction between the election outcome (the repudiation of a progressive reform program) and her prior exposition of the Australian penchant for social democracy fatally undermines her argument. My conclusion is: not entirely.

Others will parse this question by looking closely at the differential clustering of opinion by age, geography and demography, to ask whether segmentation manifest in different regional voting patterns can explain how a very close election result can run counter to "national" opinion (as reported by Huntley).

For my part, in trying to fathom the wreck of my own hopes, three things seem pertinent. First, one of my early mentors, the late Alan Davies, long ago explained the incoherence and inconsistency of our political outlooks, describing them as like a DIY project where we fashion a response "good enough" to satisfy a particular need, then put that aside until another challenge arises, when we might adopt something different, building up an assemblage of contradictory elements that we can draw on when prompted, but that we never squarely address (see his *Skills, Outlooks and Passions*, 1980). Different events will then elicit disparate responses (the question of a survey researcher on climate change, versus the task of deciding a vote, for instance). So it becomes possible for an individual to believe that action on climate change is needed, yet to vote for a party that shows little potential for action because a supervening belief (on sound economic management, for instance) is called forth.

Second, Chris Achen and Larry Bartels (*Democracy for Realists*, 2016) have shown convincingly that voting decisions are driven not by assessments of evidence and policy, but by group identity, emotion and a search for cues from those one regards as "people like us." Thus, even Liberal supporters, well removed from the inner circles of party activism, closer to mainstream opinion and inclined to support climate action (Huntley notes that 60 per cent of Coalition voters are in this category), once in the voting booth will nevertheless succumb to the emotional pull of party identity and bridle at voting against "people like us."

Third, one of the pioneers of opinion research, Walter Lippmann, nearly a century ago, warned us to be wary of "the phantom public" in a book of that title (1925). There is, he argued, no "public" out there waiting to be tapped; rather "publics" are created by political mobilisation, triggered by insiders for their own ends. They are emergent rather than stable entities, continually evolving in response to political action and representation. Thus Tony Abbott, always ready with simplifying binaries, articulates the crucial factor in how belief around climate change was mobilised in the 2019 campaign: "Where climate change is a moral issue, we Liberals do it tough. But where climate change is an economic issue the Liberals do well." The responses Huntley records might well be construed as answers to a normative question: "What should we do?" But the actions of voters on the day can be thought of as an evaluation of economic interests. The Coalition, in successfully mobilising climate action as an economic issue, created a countervailing "public" to that which Huntley and others thought representative of the zeitgeist.

James Walter

Carol Johnson

In *Australia Fair*, Rebecca Huntley provides an insightful analysis of the mood of the nation, arguing that in many respects Australians already occupy a social-democratic space – one informed by values of fairness and compassion, as well as concern about issues such as climate change. Labor's positive strategy in its 2019 election campaign suggested that it shared a similar analysis of the public's support for progressive change. Indeed, if Labor had won, Huntley would have given a far more profound analysis of why than any other commentator.

As it turned out, Huntley provides an analysis that explains a great deal about the Coalition's strategy. Faced with such a zeitgeist, it is not surprising that the Liberals' best answer was to try to instil a fear of change, relying on arguments that Labor's policies would wreck the economy, that ordinary Australians would be crippled by Labor's higher "taxes," and that properties would lose their value while rents would rise. The Liberals claimed they were already tackling climate change but in economically responsible ways, while Labor's policies would destroy jobs and incomes, increase energy costs and even take away the tradie's ute and the family car. No wonder, too, that the Liberals denied making substantial cuts to health and education and walked away from former treasurer Joe Hockey's explicit rhetoric attacking citizens' entitlements. Scott Morrison stated that there would be "a fair go for those who have a go."

Overall, the Coalition was offering more of the same while Labor was arguing that things could not stay the same – that Australians need an economy and society that are environmentally sound, fairer and more inclusive. Huntley challenged Labor to listen to the nation and gain Australians' trust. If Labor had won the 2019 election, she argued that an incoming Labor government should have seized the opportunities offered, both keeping its promises and developing an even more ambitious agenda. Labor should have been "bold," "unapologetic" and "courageous."

That Labor program was not to be, at least at this election. The Coalition's framing of the issues, and its related scare campaign, won the day. It was Labor that was construed as unfair to ordinary voters ranging from retirees to home owners. The risks of change were construed as being greater than the risks of sticking with the political status quo. However, it should be noted that future governments, whether Liberal or Labor, are likely to face significant difficulties in managing the winds of change and in keeping the electorate's trust. Australia's economy is one that will neither stay the same nor be easy to make fairer. Climate change is only one of many difficult challenges that need to be faced. Australia will also have to negotiate both the Asian Century and technological disruption and, above all, the interactions of the two.

As I explain in my new book, *Social Democracy and the Crisis of Equality: Australian Social Democracy in Changing Times*, a future Labor government committed to increasing equality would face significant issues. Successive Australian governments have tended to depict the rise of Asian economies largely in positive terms: for example, as opening up amazing new markets for Australian goods and services as the Asian middle class grows. There are indeed major new opportunities; however, there is also increasing competition from goods and services produced in those countries, with implications for Australian jobs and incomes.

Unfortunately, technological disruption is increasing some negative impacts – for example, by facilitating the off-shoring of work in Australia to employees with lower pay and conditions overseas. While offshoring once mainly affected blue-collar workers in manufacturing or white-collar workers in call centres, it now also affects skilled workers in areas such as accounting, graphic design and law. For example, financial services companies are being offered packages in the Philippines or India in which highly skilled workers process financial data for as little as $7 or $12 an hour (and without the employer having to pay costs such as superannuation or payroll tax). In the longer term, Australian workers in areas ranging from mining to service delivery do not just face being replaced by local algorithms and robots – commentators such as Richard Baldwin suggest they could be replaced by lower-paid overseas employees working virtually onshore using telerobotics and telepresence.

Importantly, classic social-democratic measures such as investing in improving skills and training would not be sufficient to deal with such problems, given that Australian workers would not only be competing with highly skilled, and often English-speaking, workers from overseas, but also with ever smarter machines. Labor governments would certainly need to introduce bolder, more courageous and more imaginative policies.

Coalition governments might not be quite so concerned about some of the industrial relations and other equity issues as Labor would be. Indeed, Joe Hockey once argued that Australia could not afford some of its current welfare benefits, given the competition from Asian countries that spent a lower proportion of their GDP on welfare. However, all Australian governments would be concerned about potentially negative impacts on the Australian economy and their flow-on effects.

In the longer-term best case, the underlying zeitgeist Huntley describes may be able to be harnessed to support government measures that address these challenges in ways that do contribute to a fairer Australia. The many benefits of geo-economic change could be made to outweigh the downsides. Australians could even extend their concerns about fairness to the pay and conditions of workers overseas. Hope could triumph over fear. In the worst case, the social-democratic ethos may not withstand the joint pressures of social and economic change. We may see a less generous and more divided nation emerge that has lost faith in the ability of government to support and protect citizens.

The challenges for governments wishing to provide a better future are therefore substantial ones, and likely to become even more so in the coming years. Whether Australian politicians of any political persuasion are up to the task remains to be seen.

Carol Johnson

AUSTRALIA FAIR

Correspondence

Travers McLeod

At the heart of Rebecca Huntley's *Australia Fair* is the idea that we are a nation of democrats. Our affinity with democracy is much more than the process of voting to elect a government. It is our collective desire for a confident democracy, with government as an active and effective partner, and a fairer society where all Australians can live flourishing lives.

This is a powerful idea in an essay that I felt was spot-on in its claim that "there is an opportunity to renew social democracy, Australian-style." The Centre for Policy Development's research, which Huntley cites, discovered an Australian appetite for democratic and policy renewal, along with broad agreement on the direction of travel. We found that Australians believe democracy is a force for fairness and equality and would throw their support behind changes that get government and the economy working better for the community.

The federal election result does not disprove Huntley's core claim. Elections are about placing trust in a person and a party to respond to the biggest problems and the greatest opportunities of our time. A clear set of ideas and policies can help to build trust. Ideas can also sow distrust and division. The election confirmed that citizens remain profoundly divided on the best path forward for the nation. But I am willing to believe, as Centre for Policy Development research shows, that all Australians share a desire to improve the lives of others and tackle our biggest problems together.

Many conservatives have forgotten the point Robert Menzies made in October 1942, when he said that Australians "disagree among ourselves on almost every conceivable subject, but we are all democrats." Menzies said our "most grievous error" has been to think "too much of democracy in mechanical terms." He also said, somewhat ominously, that "if, as a voter, I am concerned only with my own advantage and am indifferent to the cost to others, I am simply corrupt. I am selling my vote for an individual mess of pottage."

Truth be told, most Australians have equated national politics in Canberra with a thick stew. The pressure-cooker environment of the past decade has produced an enormous gap between what Australians want from their democracy and what it has delivered. More than two-thirds of Australians told CPD that they do not believe their elected representatives serve their interests. Three-quarters believe politics is fixated on short-term gains instead of long-term challenges. They are not sure government will help to look after them, their families and their communities over the long term.

In April, Gabrielle Chan reported for *The Guardian* on the fury in Farrer, an electorate in country New South Wales stretching along the Murray River from Wentworth to Albury. The source of the fury was water, or the lack of it, in a land beset by drought. Months earlier, the South Australian Murray-Darling Royal Commission had described the "do-nothing" conduct of the senior management and the board of the Murray-Darling Basin Authority in relation to climate change as "negligent" and "unlawful." Farrer didn't fall to an independent, as some thought it might, but there was a swing of almost 10 per cent against the sitting member.

I spent six months in Albury in 2017. What struck me was how different the conversation about climate change was on Dean Street in Albury, compared to the rhetoric a few hundred kilometres up the road in Canberra. What the locals in Albury couldn't stand most of all was being treated like mugs – taken for granted or ignored in the national conversation. Tellingly, it was a road trip from Sydney to Adelaide via Deniliquin, a town near the Murray River, that the Reserve Bank's deputy governor, Guy Debelle, used to frame his landmark speech about climate change and the economy in March this year. Describing climate change as a "trend" change likely to have "first-order" economic effects, Dr Debelle said:

> The transition path poses challenges, but it also presents opportunities. Particular industries and particular communities that are especially exposed to the costs of changes in the climate will face lower costs if there is an early and orderly transition. Others will bear greater costs from the transition to a lower carbon economy. While others still, such as the renewables sector, may benefit from that transition. But unlike the example of trade, it may not be possible for the winners to compensate the losers in a way that leaves no-one worse off.

The election result has not washed away these problems. They will become more acute. The murkiness of the Murray-Darling Basin Authority and water buybacks is one thing. The lack of a coherent national strategy on climate change is another. Bizarrely, compelling evidence in support of constructive policy change does not lead to political action. But inaction like this is not limited to climate change.

Instead of climate change, consider "jobs" as an example. In the 2018 December quarter, the unemployment rate in Albury City was 9.26 per cent, more than double the overall rate in New South Wales. That same month, the report *I Want to Work: Employment Services 2020* was released by the then federal minister for jobs, Kelly O'Dwyer. This expert review of *jobactive*, Australia's $6.5 billion employment services system, consulted more than 1400 jobseekers, employers, employment services providers and community groups. Its blunt assessment was that Australia "can do better. Much better." Consultant-to-client ratios were 1:148. Only 4 per cent of Australian employers were using *jobactive* in 2018 (down from 18 per cent in 2007). The system was failing a large majority of jobseekers who had been on the books for twelve months or more.

Given that outsourced delivery contracts for *jobactive* were due to expire in 2020, here was a great opportunity to think big, act on expert advice and embrace local solutions that were fit for purpose. To build an employment services program in Albury, for example, that was designed to meet the needs of that community. The response? Apart from two trials, the can was kicked further down the road. Shortly before the federal election was announced, Minister O'Dwyer extended existing *jobactive* contracts for a further two years, to the middle of 2022. One of 2019's biggest policy reform opportunities sank with barely a ripple. Providers damned in a national review won contracts for another two years. Our most disadvantaged jobseekers lost out – again. A thick stew indeed.

Huntley's essay tells us that Australians do not want to do away with democracy. We want to save it. The big question is: how?

Just as Australian democrats value substance over style, so it goes that ideas developed with local communities will matter as much as national reforms to systems and processes. Good democracies are stable. But they are not static. Nostalgia, whether it be for the reform era of the 1980s and '90s (vale Bob Hawke) or the sanctity of our Anglo-American alliances, will not help Australia to grow and decarbonise our economy, create secure jobs, find our way in Asia, build an education nation, achieve equal rights for women and give substance to the Uluru Statement from the Heart. Blind faith in markets, microeconomics and outsourced services will not elevate the public interest above shareholder interest. Put simply, the "good society" in the twenty-first century does not resemble the "good society" of last century. It is, Huntley writes powerfully, "there for the making."

What is the point of Australia? Ben Chifley famously described one "great objective – the light on the hill," which he defined as striving for the betterment of humankind not just in Australia but anywhere we may give a helping hand. Huntley offers another, built on the Australian Settlement, which is to solve big problems. She spruiks the strong social licence to act that governments often gain when Australians are convinced that "something is harmful to the collective good." She also makes it clear that some of these challenges, not least climate change, will require "the kind of mobilisation of people and communities, assets and resources, governments and infrastructure usually reserved for a world war."

Too often, attempts to galvanise communities around big challenges are done half-heartedly. As the Harvard University political scientist John Ruggie said on a visit to Australia in April, "If they're not with you at take-off, they won't be there when you land." "Community deals" to boost economic and social inclusion, built from backbone institutions at the local level and based on place-based approaches, are a way forward. They can be used to tackle disadvantage and the inevitable transitioning of coal communities to new industries and opportunities. But they require honesty about the change ahead and genuine agency for affected communities to find hope and aspiration in a frank conversation about their future. We must be able to talk positively about what we hope to start in regional Australia, not simply what we want to stop, and bring everyone along on that journey.

The chance to mobilise Australia around new, bold missions was precisely why the Centre for Policy Development brought Mariana Mazzucato to Australia last year. Mazzucato's work on public value and the entrepreneurial state doesn't pit government against business, unions or the community. What it does provide is a framework for us all to agree on missions that we can have a crack at together. Achieving them would engage the long-held ambition Australians have for their democracy as a force for equality and help to satisfy their disposition to put growth on a smarter, more inclusive and more sustainable path.

Travers McLeod

AUSTRALIA
FAIR

Correspondence

Isabelle Reinecke

Rebecca Huntley was right. The polls can be wrong. But so are many of the federal election hot takes.

Huntley, in her excellent essay *Australia Fair*, described the Australia many of us know and experience every day. Australia isn't a backward place, governed by fear. We don't have an aversion to expertise and science. We do apply a sense of fairness to our communities and people in need of our protection. We are no longer the parochial Australia of the Menzies era, and we are much more progressive than some would have us believe.

Centre for Policy Development research found that significant numbers of Australians – between 30 and 50 per cent, depending on demographic variables – believe that the purpose of Australian democracy is to "ensure that all people are treated fairly and equally, including the most vulnerable in the community." As Huntley says, social research "taken together gives a consistent and reliable picture of where the majority of Australians sit." This research shows shared values of a large majority of Australians *across party lines* for everything from renewable energy, ABC and NDIS funding, child care and housing affordability, education reforms and the Uluru Statement from the Heart. The 2019 federal election result was not a mainstream repudiation of these values; at least in part, it was a reflection of the broad public distrust in political parties and a cynicism about their ability to deliver competently on these issues.

Huntley says that this lack of trust in politicians has damaged social democracy, and we know from Lowy Polls that while 77 per cent of people aged over sixty believe democracy is the best form of governance available, only 49 per cent of young people aged eighteen to twenty-nine agree.

So what do we do when trust in democracy is so low? Huntley says if we are to renew democracy, we can't just change policies, we must reform the way politicians and parties operate.

Concentrated media ownership, donations that channel large amounts of capital into campaigns that promote the interests of a few – think of the tens of million spent by the mining lobby against the Minerals Resources Rent Tax in 2012, or the $60 million spent by Clive Palmer in the 2019 election – and of course the offer of a nice cushy corporate "government relations" job for pollies upon retirement – all these things need to change now.

But I'd argue that this renewal needs to reach beyond the executive and legislature; it also needs to encompass that oft-forgotten third pillar: the judiciary. Essential Media reports that the High Court is our second-most trusted institution, after the police. Conveniently, it is also our democracy's in-built accountability mechanism and a pathway to renewing that democracy.

Following the seminal *Mabo*, *Wik* and implied freedom of political communication decisions in the 1990s, the High Court and its leaders were subjected to ruthless public attacks by vested interests in the conservative media and those determined to limit the court's ability to act as a check on government power.

To undermine this ability – and law-driven judgments – the bench was painted as an anti-democratic institution of elites, copying a framing successfully used in the United States. This was an attempt by farming and mining industries and conservative politicians to maintain the status quo, to ensure that their pathways to power through political donations and lobbying remained intact, and to push back on a court that was playing its democratically mandated role to act as a check on the power of government and corporations.

In a lot of ways, this campaign was successful. In what may be an effort to protect themselves from these attacks, Australian superior courts can be – in the words of the distinguished former South African constitutional court justice Albie Sachs – "erudite, but incredibly technical" in their decision-making style. This has played out in recent cases, including the High Court's refusal to decide whether an Australian lesbian mother had standing to bring a case challenging the marriage equality plebiscite. It continues to play out in the court's reluctance to hear cases that might lead to the reopening of *Al-Kateb* (an infamous 2004 decision that has enabled the government to hold vulnerable people in detention indefinitely).

It played out in the refusal – in a world of mass migration and in a country with a long history of immigration – to implement a practical interpretation of Section 44 of the constitution, leading to a suite of resignations and even a by-election that ultimately led to the re-election of Barnaby Joyce, whom the court had deemed to be invalidly elected despite being born in Tamworth and his father, a New Zealander, becoming a naturalised Australian citizen in 1978.

This isn't our only problem. The unchecked power of money is not only corrupting our politics, but also hindering the ability of citizens to hold government and corporate power to account. Without their ability to use the courts as a check, our democracy is forced to limp along, lopsided. One of the biggest problems for public-interest litigants hoping to hold the powerful to account is the huge financial gamble plaintiffs must take to bring a case. Even with pro bono lawyers, the threat of an adverse costs order that can reach into the many millions is prohibitive. It stops actions before they start but does nothing to inhibit corporations that can claim these costs as a tax deduction.

Usually in Australia, adverse cost orders are decided at the end of cases to cover some of the costs of the winning party – which sounds fair when you're two construction companies tussling over a development, but not quite so fair when you're a lesbian mother keen to ask the court on behalf of her community to determine whether a marriage equality plebiscite is legal; or if you're a group of suburban doctors asking the court to decide whether Border Force gag laws on health professionals working in Manus and Nauru breach the implied freedom of political communication. The results of a loss can be financially catastrophic.

This huge financial burden deters people from bringing public interest cases based on ideas that underpin our concept of Australian social democracy: the fair treatment of the most vulnerable in our community and their equal treatment under the law.

Australia is an outlier here. JusticeConnect estimates that 90 per cent of meritorious cases are not reaching the court because of the burden of adverse costs. While researching the subject on a Churchill Fellowship in 2017, I found that Australia's system is uniquely punitive in public interest cases, even compared with that of the UK. The fact that citizens can't bring such cases free from fear of crippling bankruptcy is a procedural quirk of the Australian legal system that must be addressed as a priority. It sounds a bit boring, but it is absolutely vital that we address this financial imbalance in access to the courts. Unless we can renew all three pillars of democracy, we have little hope of creating the lasting renewal that we all crave.

Isabelle Reinecke

Response to Correspondence

Rebecca Huntley

Usually, the author's response to Quarterly Essay correspondence gratefully accepts praise given, addresses criticisms levelled and reflects on anything that has happened since the essay was published, building further on the central thesis. But I think we can accept that this is an unusual moment in Australian political history. And so I will use my right of reply as a chance to review what I wrote in January and outline my initial reaction to the results of the election, addressing the generous and insightful responses as I go.

In the essay, I talked at some length about how much we can trust public opinion polls. I wrote:

> My profession has been under attack for many years as contributing to the corruption and mendacity of party politics. Not only are our methods questioned, and the ways in which our work is used criticised, but the veracity of our conclusions is constantly doubted. It's common for commentators to say on election night that the polls got it wrong. While it is true that some polling (namely, seat-based robo-polling) can be unreliable, there is no evidence that national political polls in Australia are inaccurate. In fact, history shows that such polls produce exceptionally accurate results, even with the transition from landlines to mobile phones and online surveys over the past decade or so.

While this statement was based on the evidence available at the time, it's clear that I placed too much faith in the methods of pollsters in Australia and the extent to which compulsory voting had buffered our national polls from the kinds of inaccuracies exposed by Brexit and Trump. The reality is that our fetish for polls never made much sense. Polling never told us the full story, because the act of voting is a very blunt tool to measure the complexities of public sentiment.

However, we can't let this polling fail license a retreat to "anecdotalism"; polling data will still play a role in the mix of different kinds of information that help inform strategy. That being said, there is no sugar-coating the immediate impact of all this on my profession's reputation. Political polling represents about 1 per cent of social and market research, but it is the research that gets the most attention. The election result presents a challenge to all polling and research agencies to come up with new tools to understand how the public feel about politics and policy. However, there may be one very good outcome from this result: that we care less about published polling, that journalists talk about polls less and politicians refer to them less.

Just because I am not a pollster doesn't mean I haven't had cause to reflect on my methods. I trusted the polls and the fact that the trend consistently favoured Labor shaped my expectation in the essay that Australians were responding favourably to Labor's plan for government. When I started my career, I came to understand the Australian community through a unique research project that no longer exists, the Ipsos *Mind & Mood Report*. It involved a highly intelligent and empathetic group of women working as a team, travelling around Australia, listening to groups of friends and colleagues talk very broadly about how they felt about their lives, their families, their communities and the direction of the country. We visited homes, workplaces, garages, classrooms, cafes and community centres. I haven't conducted research like that for about four years. Instead, the research I have undertaken has been on very specific issues. So it's no surprise I missed the meta-sentiment. Marc Stears, director of the Sydney Policy Lab at the University of Sydney and former speechwriter for British Labour's Ed Milliband, wrote that people vote on overall feel and rarely on individual policies; the more you have actual conversations with people, the more apparent that is. To quote a classic Australian movie, it's the vibe. So as a researcher, I have recommitted myself to more listening, to asking more open questions of people, to reconnecting with the vibe.

As I write this, we are still in the swirl of analysis about what happened and why. Some of it is intelligent and thought-provoking, some of it is not. Views range from "nothing much has shifted" to "everything we know to be true is not." The correct interpretation must lie somewhere in the middle. I certainly have more questions than answers at the moment, but I also have a few thoughts worth sharing. One wise head told me on election night that for Labor (in particular) to win federally, all the elements need to line up – a strong leader, a strong campaign and the right policy settings to fit the mood of the electorate. All those elements might not have been equal contributors to the party's election loss, but they all need to be considered in its wake.

In the essay, I underestimated the importance of the leader. I recalled people voting for a leader they didn't particularly like in Tony Abbott and thought the same logic would work for Bill Shorten. Perhaps the more disengaged and anxious voters are, the more the leader matters, particularly to the undecided. Given Labor was promising a suite of complex policies, the likeability of the leader and the strength of the campaign became even more important. Understanding what works and doesn't work in a campaign is not my forte, but what I didn't consider in the essay was whether Labor's agenda (even though it dovetailed nicely with what the majority of Australians say they want) could withstand the negative campaigning and misinformation that was thrown at it. Finally, what I outlined in the essay was a policy agenda for a popular Labor government rather than a policy platform to win an election. The question I didn't ask myself was this: how does the progressive centre of sentiment hold up when those sentiments are translated into policy and sold to an anxious public? The idea that Australia is trending to the right doesn't line up with political reality: Labor governments in Queensland and Western Australia as well as the more progressive Victoria. The results in South Australia, with a conservative state government in power, saw a two-party-preferred split of 56/44 in favour of Labor. While the majority of Australians support progressive policies in the social-democratic tradition when presented with them in surveys and focus groups, the challenge progressive parties face is this: how to sell that to people during a campaign, when trust in politics is so low? And so I wouldn't be surprised if what Labor campaigners take out of this loss is that to win campaigns you need a strong, likeable leader, a small-target policy strategy and a generous side-serve of fear about the alternative.

The essay made an argument that there is a progressive centre in Australian society and that the foundations exist for a revived social democracy with environmental concerns at its core. Yet Labor fell short and I underestimated the impact of a few issues. The first of these is tax. As I said in the essay, tax reform is where the rubber hits the road when it comes to revitalising social democracy. Will voters cop modest tax increases if it means more spending on the services they consistently say they want? I made the point that when it comes to a possible loss in one area in exchange for gains in another, trust becomes essential. You have to trust the party in government to do as it says it will: to take and give rather than just take. But the reaction to Labor's tax reform ideas also prompts a broader, more nuanced discussion about our attitudes to fairness. Of course, our concept of fairness is pretty malleable. And we are, overall, an affluent country. So did people think it was unfair to take franking credits away? And was that perception of unfairness enough to provide fertile ground for a scare campaign on a retiree tax and a death tax? As Carol Johnson comments, "it was Labor that was construed as unfair to ordinary voters ranging from retirees to home owners." (It should be noted that negative gearing policies didn't seem to hurt Labor in 2016, so perhaps the focus on franking credits was taken as an attack on those aged over sixty-five, a sizeable part of the voting population.) Again, I think one of the lessons for Labor campaigners must be that it's only in government that you are able to show that the politics of economic redistribution are possible, that your kind of government will give more to the vast majority of citizens in return for modest tax reform. And that, ironically, the language of all-out class warfare can backfire in a "classless" society like Australia, even when social inequality is becoming more pronounced.

The second issue is climate change. The ballot box has always been an imprecise tool for measuring public sentiment on complex issues, especially ones that provoke the spectrum of emotion in us as climate change does – fear, denial, guilt, anxiety, anger and hope. This was the climate election, but not in the way people (including myself) thought it would be. Again, I looked to the past to predict the future; concern about climate helped Labor in 2007. Climate change concern was a reason why the Liberal Party lost Warringah and an independent held on in Indi. It was one of the reasons we saw swings away from the Liberals in seats like North Sydney. But results for the LNP in Queensland and even One Nation in the Hunter show a swing in the opposite direction in parts of Australia where mining jobs are being threatened and where workers don't feel they can be nimble in response to a changing economy. I said in the essay that I thought that as a community we were inching towards recognition of the scale of the climate threat. In fact, if the election result is any kind of gauge, while some parts of our society are quickly moving in that direction, other parts may be pushing back. Griffith University academics Anne Tiernan, Jacob Deem and Jennifer Menzies argue that the results in Queensland reflect a decentralised and highly local reaction to the "climate change versus coal" equation.

> Putting to one side the fact that the swings against Labor were not much bigger in Queensland than some other parts of the country, and that it had the most marginal seats in the election, the instinct to blame and deride Queensland highlights exactly what went wrong for the ALP … Queenslanders are not all deeply conservative, rusted-on LNP voters, even in central and northern regions. Instead, the federal Labor Party, like the many pundits who predicted an ALP win, seem to have underestimated or misunderstood

> the variances and nuances of the Queensland electorate. As the only state where a majority of the population lives outside the capital city, regionalism matters in Queensland in a way it does not elsewhere.

As Travers McLeod points out, Australians are not sure government will look after them, their families and their communities over the long term. Perhaps this is particularly so in regional communities struggling to survive. And so they respond to appeals that focus on local jobs over those that focus on the "national interest." All politics is local but some politics is more local than others.

The election result also makes me reflect on where exactly the community is on climate. Beneath the top-line figures that point to consensus, there are schisms that are going to be hard to shift. Susan Carland writes that "we are living in a time of profound social silos and tribalism." James Walter makes a similar point, saying that we need to be wary of "the phantom public" and instead understand there are various "publics" that are "created by political mobilisation, triggered by insiders for their own ends." Interestingly, while I didn't anticipate the election result, in my work on attitudes to climate change I have been coming to the realisation that the approaches to understanding sentiment on climate and therefore the strategies to mobilise climate action are inadequate. My current research, which will eventually be a book, is on climate change and emotion and how individual and group psychology should inform how those in the climate change movement communicate and persuade.

To reiterate, I don't think Australia is inherently an ideologically conservative nation. I do think it may well be a temperamentally conservative one. This result doesn't mean we are right-wing. It means we are scared. We want change desperately, but we are equally scared of change when it involves trusting the political system to bring it about. So politically we are stuck, at a time when so much else – in the economy, society and environment – is moving quickly.

One area I spent a lot of time exploring in the essay is the lack of trust in politics. All the responses address this in their own way. Isabelle Reinecke wrote that the election result is not a repudiation of progressive values but a reflection of deep cynicism about the ability of political parties to deliver competently on these issues. If I were to write my essay again, it would be focused through the lens of public distrust of politics, because if there is one big message coming from this election result, it is that despite our voting record Australians are alienated from the system. Before anyone speculates on how people responded to Labor's policies, they first need to ask: were people listening much in the first place? There are signs they weren't. The high number of pre-poll votes, 4.7 million in this election, was driven by our desire for convenience, but must also reflect that people had made up their minds before the campaign started and wanted to block the whole blasted business out. Not exactly an environment for change. And the cynicism about the two major parties continued unabated. In my essay, I outlined the decline of public trust in institutions and our growing despair about politics and politicians. I pointed to the increasing number of younger people wondering if Australian democracy can deliver on its promise. In an election where there was in fact a stark choice in policy, there was still the prevailing "they are both the same as each other" sentiment. Many independents did well, capitalising on negative feelings about the two parties. And contrary to so many predictions (not mine), scandal after scandal didn't do much to the One Nation vote and delivered votes for Clive Palmer, even in a place like Townsville, where he still owes people money.

Indeed, the irony is that Labor was the most stable and united team on the ballot: the Liberals, Nationals, Greens and One Nation were all involved in very public, ugly fights in the twelve months leading up to the election, even during the campaign itself. (The United Australia Party wasn't even a party but an electoral scaffold for a scare campaign aimed at Bill Shorten so that Clive Palmer could advance his interests in the Galilee Basin.) Disunity may no longer be death if the voters assume you are all a rabble. What this says to me is that we need to explore different ways for Australians to get involved in public decision-making, not just the kinds of deliberative-democracy mechanisms I mentioned in my essay but also the community organising that was successful in seats like Indi. It's a lesson too for the major political parties, that internal party reform is as important as ever and that "politics as usual" will deliver lower and lower numbers of primary votes.

On social media, I've watched Labor and Greens supporters lash out at Queenslanders and other Australians who voted for the status quo, calling them stupid, lazy, racist and selfish. The cynicism about the electorate from some parts of the left never goes away. The conclusion to draw is not that Australia is no longer progressive or no longer cares about equality or is becoming like America, or that all social research lacks credibility. The conclusion is that the lack of trust the electorate has in politics has undermined its belief that structural reform – whether that be economic, social or environmental – is something that can be delivered by the politicians running the show. That is especially the case when some kind of exchange is being promised – more tax for better services.

The challenge is to take what the majority of Australians want and connect that with a government they feel comfortable electing. The alternative is a race to the bottom, with campaigns run on slogans about fear and the status quo, allowing no possibility of reform. That's not what the nation needs, or what it consistently says it wants outside the ballot box. The task for progressives is to build trust, from the ground up, that what we need and want can actually be delivered by the politics we have.

I remain a defiant optimist. Just one who now recognises the scale of the challenge ahead.

Rebecca Huntley

Susan Carland's first book was *Fighting Hislam*. She is the director of the Bachelor of Global Studies at Monash University and hosts the SBS quiz show *Child Genius*.

Rebecca Huntley is one of Australia's foremost social researchers. From 2006 until 2015, she was the director of the *Mind & Mood Report*, Australia's longest-running social trends report. She is now head of Vox Populi research. Her most recent book is *Still Lucky*.

Erik Jensen is the award-winning author of *Acute Misfortune* and *On Kate Jennings*. He is founding editor of *The Saturday Paper* and editor-in-chief of Schwartz Media. He has written for film and television, and was the winner of the Walkley Award for Young Print Journalist of the Year and the United Nations Association of Australia's Media Peace Award.

Carol Johnson is an adjunct professor in politics and international relations at the University of Adelaide. She is the author of *Social Democracy and the Crisis of Equality* and *The Labor Legacy*.

Travers McLeod is CEO of the Centre for Policy Development, an Australian policy institute.

Isabelle Reinecke is executive director and founder of Grata Fund. She has worked as a solicitor at Clayton Utz in Sydney and as legal and governance director at GetUp.

James Walter is emeritus professor of politics at Monash University. His latest book is *The Pivot of Power: Australian Prime Ministers and Political Leadership, 1949–2016* (with Paul Strangio and Paul 't Hart).

QUARTERLY ESSAY BACK ISSUES

BACK ISSUES: (Prices include GST, postage and handling within Australia.)

- ☐ **QE 1** ($15.99) Robert Manne *In Denial*
- ☐ **QE 2** ($15.99) John Birmingham *Appeasing Jakarta*
- ☐ **QE 3** ($15.99) Guy Rundle *The Opportunist*
- ☐ **QE 4** ($15.99) Don Watson *Rabbit Syndrome*
- ☐ **QE 5** ($15.99) Mungo MacCallum *Girt By Sea*
- ☐ **QE 6** ($15.99) John Button *Beyond Belief*
- ☐ **QE 7** ($15.99) John Martinkus *Paradise Betrayed*
- ☐ **QE 8** ($15.99) Amanda Lohrey *Groundswell*
- ☐ **QE 9** ($15.99) Tim Flannery *Beautiful Lies*
- ☐ **QE 10** ($15.99) Gideon Haigh *Bad Company*
- ☐ **QE 11** ($15.99) Germaine Greer *Whitefella Jump Up*
- ☐ **QE 12** ($15.99) David Malouf *Made in England*
- ☐ **QE 13** ($15.99) Robert Manne with David Corlett *Sending Them Home*
- ☐ **QE 14** ($15.99) Paul McGeough *Mission Impossible*
- ☐ **QE 15** ($15.99) Margaret Simons *Latham's World*
- ☐ **QE 16** ($15.99) Raimond Gaita *Breach of Trust*
- ☐ **QE 17** ($15.99) John Hirst *'Kangaroo Court'*
- ☐ **QE 18** ($15.99) Gail Bell *The Worried Well*
- ☐ **QE 19** ($15.99) Judith Brett *Relaxed & Comfortable*
- ☐ **QE 20** ($15.99) John Birmingham *A Time for War*
- ☐ **QE 21** ($15.99) Clive Hamilton *What's Left?*
- ☐ **QE 22** ($15.99) Amanda Lohrey *Voting for Jesus*
- ☐ **QE 23** ($15.99) Inga Clendinnen *The History Question*
- ☐ **QE 24** ($15.99) Robyn Davidson *No Fixed Address*
- ☐ **QE 25** ($15.99) Peter Hartcher *Bipolar Nation*
- ☐ **QE 26** ($15.99) David Marr *His Master's Voice*
- ☐ **QE 27** ($15.99) Ian Lowe *Reaction Time*
- ☐ **QE 28** ($15.99) Judith Brett *Exit Right*
- ☐ **QE 29** ($15.99) Anne Manne *Love & Money*
- ☐ **QE 30** ($15.99) Paul Toohey *Last Drinks*
- ☐ **QE 31** ($15.99) Tim Flannery *Now or Never*
- ☐ **QE 32** ($15.99) Kate Jennings *American Revolution*
- ☐ **QE 33** ($15.99) Guy Pearse *Quarry Vision*
- ☐ **QE 34** ($15.99) Annabel Crabb *Stop at Nothing*
- ☐ **QE 35** ($15.99) Noel Pearson *Radical Hope*
- ☐ **QE 36** ($15.99) Mungo MacCallum *Australian Story*
- ☐ **QE 37** ($15.99) Waleed Aly *What's Right?*
- ☐ **QE 38** ($15.99) David Marr *Power Trip*
- ☐ **QE 39** ($15.99) Hugh White *Power Shift*
- ☐ **QE 40** ($15.99) George Megalogenis *Trivial Pursuit*
- ☐ **QE 41** ($15.99) David Malouf *The Happy Life*
- ☐ **QE 42** ($15.99) Judith Brett *Fair Share*
- ☐ **QE 43** ($15.99) Robert Manne *Bad News*
- ☐ **QE 44** ($15.99) Andrew Charlton *Man-Made World*
- ☐ **QE 45** ($15.99) Anna Krien *Us and Them*
- ☐ **QE 46** ($15.99) Laura Tingle *Great Expectations*
- ☐ **QE 47** ($15.99) David Marr *Political Animal*
- ☐ **QE 48** ($15.99) Tim Flannery *After the Future*
- ☐ **QE 49** ($15.99) Mark Latham *Not Dead Yet*
- ☐ **QE 50** ($15.99) Anna Goldsworthy *Unfinished Business*
- ☐ **QE 51** ($15.99) David Marr *The Prince*
- ☐ **QE 52** ($15.99) Linda Jaivin *Found in Translation*
- ☐ **QE 53** ($15.99) Paul Toohey *That Sinking Feeling*
- ☐ **QE 54** ($15.99) Andrew Charlton *Dragon's Tail*
- ☐ **QE 55** ($15.99) Noel Pearson *A Rightful Place*
- ☐ **QE 56** ($15.99) Guy Rundle *Clivosaurus*
- ☐ **QE 57** ($15.99) Karen Hitchcock *Dear Life*
- ☐ **QE 58** ($15.99) David Kilcullen *Blood Year*
- ☐ **QE 59** ($15.99) David Marr *Faction Man*
- ☐ **QE 60** ($15.99) Laura Tingle *Political Amnesia*
- ☐ **QE 61** ($15.99) George Megalogenis *Balancing Act*
- ☐ **QE 62** ($15.99) James Brown *Firing Line*
- ☐ **QE 63** ($15.99) Don Watson *Enemy Within*
- ☐ **QE 64** ($15.99) Stan Grant *The Australian Dream*
- ☐ **QE 65** ($15.99) David Marr *The White Queen*
- ☐ **QE 66** ($15.99) Anna Krien *The Long Goodbye*
- ☐ **QE 67** ($15.99) Benjamin Law *Moral Panic 101*
- ☐ **QE 68** ($15.99) Hugh White *Without America*
- ☐ **QE 69** ($15.99) Mark McKenna *Moment of Truth*
- ☐ **QE 70** ($15.99) Richard Denniss *Dead Right*
- ☐ **QE 71** ($22.99) Laura Tingle *Follow the Leader*
- ☐ **QE 72** ($22.99) Sebastian Smee *Net Loss*
- ☐ **QE 73** ($22.99) Rebecca Huntley *Australia Fair*

NAME:

ADDRESS:

EMAIL: PHONE:

Please include this form with payment details on the opposite page.

FORTHCOMING ISSUES

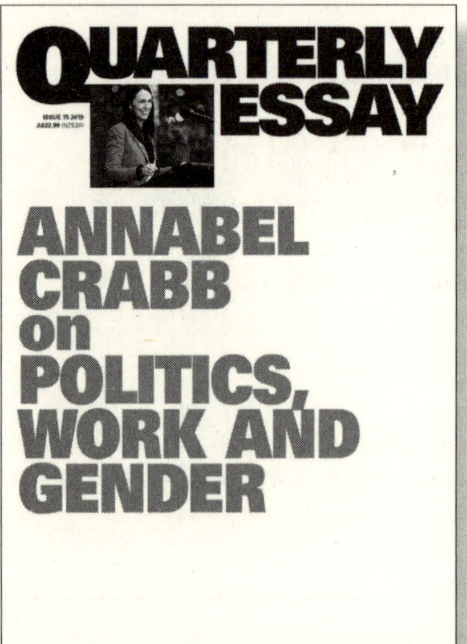

Annabel Crabb on politics, work and gender
September 2019

Annabel Crabb deploys political observation, workplace research and her characteristic humour and intelligence to argue that gender equity cannot be achieved until men are as free to leave the workplace (when their lives demand it) as women are to enter it.

Peter Hartcher on China's power and Australia's future
November 2019

In this gripping account, Peter Hartcher shows that we are entering an era of undeclared contestation, whether for hearts and minds, mineral and agricultural resources, media outlets or sea lanes. Reactions include panic, xenophobia and all-the-way-with-the-USA – but the challenge now is to think hard about the national interest and respond with wisdom to a changed world.

Please turn over for subscription order form or subscribe online at **quarterlyessay.com**
Alternatively, call 1800 077 514 or 03 9486 0244 or email subscribe@blackincbooks.com